Red Hot Chili Peppers
Californication

Matt Karpe

sonicbondpublishing.com

Sonicbond Publishing Limited
www.sonicbondpublishing.co.uk
Email: info@sonicbondpublishing.co.uk

First Published in the United Kingdom 2024
First Published in the United States 2024

British Library Cataloguing in Publication Data:
A Catalogue record for this book is available from the British Library

Copyright Matt Karpe 2024

ISBN 978-1-78952-348-5

The right of Matt Karpe to be identified
as the author of this work has been asserted by him
in accordance with the Copyright, Designs and Patents Act 1988.
All rights reserved. No part of this publication may be reproduced,
stored in a retrieval system or transmitted in any form or by any means,
electronic, mechanical, photocopying, recording or otherwise, without
prior permission in writing from Sonicbond Publishing Limited

Typeset in ITC Garamond Std & ITC Avant Garde Gothic
Printed and bound in England

Graphic design and typesetting: Full Moon Media

Follow us on social media:
Twitter: https://twitter.com/SonicbondP
Instagram: www.instagram.com/sonicbondpublishing_/
Facebook: www.facebook.com/SonicbondPublishing/

Linktree QR code:

Red Hot Chili Peppers
Californication

Matt Karpe

sonicbondpublishing.com

Preface

It was in the first quarter of the year 2000 that I began my true exploration into the world of rock music. I was 14 years old, and having only been accustomed to a bit of Bon Jovi, Guns 'N' Roses and Manic Street Preachers, I soon became fascinated with the nu metal movement. Overnight, or so it seemed, this adoptive sub-genre of sorts became such a hot topic of debate, and it was literally everywhere.

For hours on end, I would sit in front of the TV watching *Kerrang!*, taking in music video after music video from Deftones, Korn, Limp Bizkit, Slipknot and so many others. It was all so different, yet it all felt the same in a strange way – this diverse array of artists playing their own forms of metal that was often void of any tradition at all. I was, nonetheless, utterly captivated. *Kerrang!* promoted nu metal like crazy – it was the 'in thing' after all, but every so often, the channel would play videos outside of that realm. Black Sabbath, Iron Maiden, Metallica, Mötley Crüe – all stalwarts of heavy metal in one form or another. Ramones, Green Day and The Offspring were there to keep punk rock alive, while Nirvana, Pearl Jam, Alice in Chains and the Smashing Pumpkins were for lovers of grunge and those who were still struggling to come to terms with the scene's quietus.

In 1997, the British girl group All Saints released a double A-side single featuring a cover of Labelle's 'Lady Marmalade' and a second cover of a song titled 'Under The Bridge'. I remember hearing the latter on the radio at the time and being a bit of a pop fan before moving over to the dark side; I quite liked the song. I'm pretty sure I even bought the CD single. Three years later, via *Kerrang!*, I was first introduced to the Red Hot Chili Peppers. The video that came on to showcase the band to me was, of course, 'Under The Bridge'. I thought they were covering All Saints, to begin with, but I quickly realised the Chilis version was better, more powerful and painfully genuine. 'Give It Away' was also played from time to time, and then followed the videos for 'Scar Tissue' and 'Californication', given frequent rotation, day after day. Out of the five songs released as singles from *Californication*, these were the two that had the most traction in the UK.

At some point, a friend of mine bought the *Californication* album on CD. Then I borrowed it and I never gave it back. For a lover of the multifarious nature of nu metal, I was struck by the Red Hot Chili Peppers' ability to mix things up so much, from the funk-ridden exploits of 'Get On Top' and 'I Like Dirt' to the all-out rock drive of

Californication Red Hot Chili Peppers

'Around The World' and 'Parallel Universe' to the melodic progressions of 'Scar Tissue' and 'Otherside' – most of the time, the songs sharing harsh truths and honest reflections. *Californication* was my summer album for 2000, and it didn't matter that I was 12 months late to the party. I temporarily moved away from my trusted nu metal – my eyes opened to alternative rock built around finding inner peace and musical serenity. I didn't know it back then, but *Californication* would go on to be considered one of rock's greatest comeback albums and one that would turn around the fortunes of the Red Hot Chili Peppers – all I knew was that it was a great fucking record.

Many consider *Blood Sugar Sex Magik* to be the band's best LP, and *By The Way* gets a similar amount of love, but *Californication* will forever be mine. It doesn't always have to be the one that sells the most copies (in this instance, *Californication* did) or has the best set of songs, but it can sometimes simply be how that album makes you feel, how those lush guitar melodies strike a chord with you, how the lyrics hit differently or how a chorus makes you want to shout it from the rooftops. For a band in disarray in the early part of 1998, for the Red Hot Chili Peppers to be able to return with an album such as *Californication* was brave and inspiring. They even deviated into experimenting with new sounds and styles, but they did it all without ever losing their true identity.

The Chilis have multiple classic albums in their discography, but *Californication* offers the most intriguing narrative for a book. When the opportunity arose, I jumped at the chance to pay tribute to an album that is easily in my top ten of all time. But as well as paying tribute, I also wanted to evaluate and reprimand where needed because the album is not perfect by any stretch of the imagination. It has been a lot of fun digging deeper into the album than I ever had before while spinning and streaming the songs more or less on repeat for the last six months or so.

At one point or another, haven't we all dreamed of *Californication*?

Matt Karpe

Red Hot Chili Peppers
Californication

Contents

Preface 5
Introduction 9
Getting On Top 11
Dreaming Of Californication 17
Californication 23
Single Releases And Tracklistings 49
The Teatro Sessions 52
The Californication Tour 55
Reception And Commercial Performance 66
The Legacy Of Californication 70
Bibliography 74

Introduction

In August 2007, a TV series by the name of *Californication* premiered on the *Showtime* network. Starring *The X-Files* icon David Duchovny as the mercurial Hank Moody, the series followed the ups and downs of a self-loathing writer, drunk and fuck-anything-with-a-pulse kind of guy. Duchovny's portrayal of Moody was based on the great lowlife poet and author Charles Bukowski, whose famed works include the novels *Post Office* and *Ham On Rye*, who also shared a similar disdain for the city that gave him so much – Los Angeles.

The series ran for seven seasons before bowing out in 2014, and it also presented a strong focus on music. Rick Springfield, Marilyn Manson and the Wu-Tang Clan's RZA all made guest appearances in one season or another, while the show frequently used famous song and album titles for its episode headings. Some of Moody's best-sellers even bore the names of classic records, and while there never appeared to be a threat of being sued for plagiarism, it took some balls to name three of his books after some of Slayer's greatest offerings – *South Of Heaven*, *Seasons In The Abyss* and *God Hates Us All*.

Nine years before the TV show came the Red Hot Chili Peppers' seventh studio album, titled *Californication*, and it wasn't a great surprise when, in November 2007, the LA quartet filed a lawsuit against *Showtime* and the show's producers for Federal Trademark Infringement. The Chilis took exception to their album title being used in a way to compete against the band and for others to profit while also sharing concerns that fans may have been misled into thinking the show had something to do with the quartet. *Showtime* were ultimately able to avoid the suit by successfully proving the 'Californication' term dated as far back as the late 1960s, where it was used to blame the 'mindless development' of California for issues arising in communities around such states as Colorado and Oregon. Those who had abandoned the Golden State were also chastised for wanting to move to quieter areas, of which some were then considered by locals to have been 'Californicated'.

If the TV show supplied an overwhelmingly visual portrayal of California's belligerent underbelly, where drink and drugs seemingly go hand in hand, and Hollywood does its best to shatter the dreams of the young and hopeful, the Red Hot Chili Peppers had delivered their masterful soundtrack some eight years prior. Fraught, scathing, tempestuous and led by the sensational centrepiece that is the album's title track, the selection of songs found on *Californication* also displays an abundance of honesty and introspection. For a band

Californication Red Hot Chili Peppers

who had often been accused of not taking their craft seriously at that point, where their funk and punk rock hybrid was more about having fun and getting laid in their early days, *Californication* found the Red Hot Chili Peppers at a creative peak. The band members had each battled demons along the way, but as a collective, Anthony Kiedis, John Frusciante, Michal 'Flea' Balzary and Chad Smith were able to take their pain and suffering and pour it into a breathtaking and predominantly mature set of songs – all of which were made up of delicious melodies, pristine guitar work, throbbing bass, inspired drumming and rounded off by some of Kiedis' greatest lyricism.

The album isn't entirely shrouded in doom and gloom, though, and there is still a lot of fun packed into the 15 songs making up the official tracklisting. This was a new style of Red Hot Chili Peppers, though, and some were surprised to find that the band's customary funk rock approach had been set aside in favour of more mellow arrangements. But in the long run, it would prove to be the making of both the record and the band that created it. In early 1998, there were strong possibilities that the Red Hot Chili Peppers may even disband, but a year later, a revitalised quartet were beginning a new chapter, and from there on, they would never look back. This is the story of *Californication*.

Getting On Top

They say all roads lead to Hollywood, and that statement is particularly pertinent to the majority of those who, at one point or another, would be part of the Red Hot Chili Peppers.

The setting is Fairfax High School, situated at the intersection of Fairfax and Melrose Avenues and bordering West Hollywood. The year is 1977, and Anthony Kiedis is struggling to integrate with the diverse demographic of students who make up Fairfax High. And then he meets Michael Balzary, a young buck with more haywire energy than his tiny frame can burn off in one go, his scatty nature earning him the rather appropriate nickname of 'Flea'. Kiedis had arrived in Los Angeles at the age of 12, leaving behind his native Grand Rapids, Michigan, to live with his film star-wannabe father. Balzary was born in Melbourne, Australia, before being uprooted to New York City when he was just four years old. When his parents divorced a short time later, California became Balary's next destination. Seen to be uncool by many of their peers or those who actually took notice of them in the first place, Kiedis and Balzary both came from less-than-ideal home lives. This is likely why the two formed such an inimitable bond, one that would only grow through the mischief they created on the streets of LA. The bond, today reinforced by love and respect, has allowed the brothers in arms to remain the only constants in the Red Hot Chili Peppers' lineup since the band's original formation over 40 years ago.

At first, Balzary was a keen trumpeter with a penchant for jazz until he was introduced to punk rock by his friend and original Red Hot Chili Peppers guitarist Hillel Slovak. Balzary quickly learned how to play the bass guitar, where he adopted an unusual slapping technique that was as animated as the man himself. Not long after, he joined one of LA's most riotous factions, FEAR. Kiedis, on the other hand, had no musical background, having been more familiar with being in front of film cameras. While he was still in school, Kiedis scored some minor acting roles, including, most notably, the part of Sylvester Stallone's son in the 1978 neo-noir crime caper *F.I.S.T.* Kiedis' true calling wasn't too far away from revealing itself, though, because as he grew older, it was clear he possessed the charisma and confidence that made him the ideal candidate to front an aspiring rock band.

That calling came on 16 December 1982, when Kiedis' friend, Gary Allen, asked him to put together a band to play just one song at Allen's EP launch party. That night, Kiedis, Balzary, Slovak and drummer Jack Irons took to the small Grandia Room stage at the Rhythm Lounge on

Californication Red Hot Chili Peppers

Melrose Avenue for a one-time-only gig (or so it seemed at the time). They called themselves Tony Flow and the Miraculously Majestic Masters of Mayhem. Kiedis debuted an impressive rap vocal over some improvised funk and punk instrumentation, the quartet's sound a combined influence of New York's Defunkt and the hip-hop troupe of Grandmaster Flash and the Furious Five. The song Tony Flow performed on that cold December evening was titled 'Out Of L.A.', and it featured Kiedis' storytelling lyrics about his and his friends' escapades around Tinseltown after dark. The band were immediately invited back to play a slightly longer two-song set the following week. No one knew it at the time, but the early foundations of the Red Hot Chili Peppers had been laid, and before long, the quartet were playing more and more shows around the city. Their funk style was some way away from that of Mötley Crüe, Ratt and W.A.S.P., who were about to take hair metal away from the Sunset Strip and into far bigger venues, befitting of their multi-million record sales. However, with their ascent came an opportunity for new bands to come in and make an impact of their own.

By early 1983, the Red Hot Chili Peppers were officially unveiled – their name derived from those of old-school blues and jazz artists, and by the end of that year, the quartet had signed a seven-album deal with EMI America/Enigma Records. Huffing and puffing throughout the decade, the Chilis steadily built a cult following by relentlessly touring and playing shows and releasing three albums that were each chock-a-block with funk and punk party anthems. Unfortunately, drugs would play a turbulent role in the band's early years, and in a sad twist of fate, it was only when Hillel Slovak succumbed to a heroin overdose in June 1988 that the Chilis career began its upward climb.

Enter John Frusciante, an 18-year-old staunch supporter of the Red Hot Chili Peppers and a talented guitarist who already knew how to play his favourite band's songs. It may have been under desperate circumstances, but Frusciante was the natural replacement for the hugely popular Slovak, and when Chad Smith filled the vacant drummer's spot around the same time, what many consider to be the classic Red Hot Chili Peppers lineup had been founded.

The 1989 album *Mother's Milk* had Frusciante's stamp all over it, his songwriting offering a new focus on melody over rhythm. There was still a hell of a lot of funk involved, but the band's sound was clearly progressing into something more substantial and fulfilling. Within a year of release, *Mother's Milk* had earned gold certification in the US, and while the four-piece were finally on the road to bigger things, that pot of gold at the end of the rainbow would come a couple of years later in the form of *Blood Sugar Sex Magik*. Released via Warner Bros. Records on 24 September 1991, the album boasted the punchy duo of 'Give It Away' and 'Suck My Kiss', of which the former scored the Red Hot Chili Peppers their first number one on the *Billboard* Modern Rock Tracks chart. An even bigger moment came in March 1992 when the stunning heroin ballad 'Under The Bridge' was released as the second single. The song truly placed the Chilis into the mainstream, going all the way to number two on the Hot 100. With a remarkable peak position of number three on the *Billboard* 200, *Blood Sugar Sex Magik* would go on to shift over 7,000,000 copies in the US alone.

As the grunge movement began to spread its wings, future Hall of Fame acts, including Pearl Jam, Nirvana and The Smashing Pumpkins, found themselves supporting the Red Hot Chili Peppers on US tours. By the end of 1991, alternative rock was searching for some new poster boys and LA's finest foursome were in the prime position to take the mantle and run with it. Nine years after their inception, the Red Hot Chili Peppers had arrived at long last. But with success came some inevitable pitfalls. Anthony Kiedis was in and out of his own heroin addiction, as he would be on multiple occasions throughout the decade, while Flea had also become accustomed to substance abuse during his teenage years. 'I started smoking weed when I was 11, and then proceeded to snort, shoot, pop, smoke, drop and drag and chase my way through my teens and 20s', the bassist wrote during an *Opioid Diaries* series for *Time Magazine* in 2018. John Frusciante, on the other hand, was facing an entirely different struggle – with newfound fame. In Kiedis' 2005 memoir *Scar Tissue*, the frontman spoke of the guitarist's dramatic plight:

> John would say, 'We're too popular; I don't need to be at this level of success; I would just be proud to be playing this music in clubs like you guys were doing two years ago.'

Upon the completion of *Blood Sugar Sex Magik*, Frusciante tried heroin for the first time, and it would kickstart a downward spiral. Things would get worse on tour, where he and Kiedis regularly came to blows. Frusciante's mental state reached a new low when the Chilis were in Japan, and ahead of their 7 May date at Omiya Sonic City, the guitarist decided to quit the band mid-tour. Frusciante was at least convinced to play that night's show, but once it was over, he flew back to LA and became a recluse and a prolific addict. Heroin would not be the only drug on the menu. Frusciante was at least able to experience spells of creativity through drawing and painting, and he would also end up recording some solo music, releasing his first album in 1994 under the title of *Niandra LaDes And Usually Just A T-Shirt*.

To fulfil the remainder of their upcoming dates, which included a headline spot on the long summer slog of Lollapalooza, Arik Marshall was hired for guitar duties. He also featured in two music videos filmed in 1992 and toured Australia, New Zealand, Brazil and Argentina. In Kiedis' *Scar Tissue* memoir, he wrote of Marshall never letting the band down on stage. However, Marshall's final performance with the Chilis proved to be at the Grammy's on 24 February 1993. On the same night that the band won the Best Hard Rock Performance with Vocal award for 'Give It Away', the quartet played a rousing rendition of the track alongside George Clinton and Parliament-Funkadelic.

After completing the stressful *Blood Sugar Sex Magik* world tour, it was time for the Red Hot Chili Peppers to begin work on a new album, but problems arose immediately when Marshall was let go for failing to attend rehearsals. The next guitarist to come through the door was Jesse Tobias, who had been playing in and around LA with the band Mother Tongue, but his stint was cut short when Kiedis and Flea cited a lack of chemistry. Dave Navarro had been on the Chilis' radar since Frusciante's departure; in fact, they asked him to join their band before Arik Marshall came along. At the time, Navarro was dealing with his own drug issues, having recently seen his own band, Jane's Addiction, call it a day. With Tobias now gone, Navarro entered the fray, and to accommodate his heavier guitar style and the psychedelic nuances he was known for, the Red Hot Chili Peppers decided to move in a new direction for their sixth studio album. Sadly, Kiedis was back on heroin by the time work began on *One Hot Minute*, and this was after being clean for five years. The headspace all four members found themselves in played a big part in *One Hot Minute* sounding far darker and disorientating than many could have anticipated. Released in September 1995 to largely underwhelming reviews, expectations had been high after the success of *Blood Sugar Sex Magik* – even with the departure of the influential Frusciante. Despite selling over 2,000,000 copies early on and creeping inside the top five of the *Billboard* 200, *One Hot Minute* was deemed a commercial failure. The Chilis did earn another number-one hit when 'My Friends' topped the Mainstream Rock and Alternative Airplay charts, but overall, the quartet had failed to build on the momentum they had gained in the first half of the decade.

'All roads lead back home…' as the saying goes, and that is most certainly true for John Frusciante. Upon suffering a near-fatal blood infection and other ailments stemming from his persistent drug use, Frusciante eventually embarked on a successful stint in rehab. Even though he had quit the Red Hot Chili Peppers in less than auspicious circumstances, Frusciante and Flea remained in contact in the ensuing years, and it was Flea's support that allowed the guitarist to finally overcome his addictions. At the same time, the Red Hot Chili Peppers were at a serious crossroads, with talk even arising of a possible disbandment. Dave Navarro had been fired in April 1998 because of his own continuous drug issues, and in-house fighting had forced the remaining trio to retreat from one another and take some time out. With Frusciante back on the straight and narrow, it was only when Flea put forward the idea of having him rejoin the band that the Chilis career was given a shot at salvation. In an interview with *Kerrang!* in July 1999, Anthony Kiedis couldn't hide his relief at mending his relationship with Frusciante after the two hadn't spoken since the guitarist's departure back in 1992:

> It was the furthest thing from my mind that we'd ever be friends and play music again. It was beyond a dream. When it did transpire, I can say that it was a miracle shock – in a positive way. It was as close as I'll ever come to saying hello to a dead friend.

Frusciante's return felt like a miracle to most, and it was something that no one saw coming after his acrimonious departure in 1992 and the ensuing years of complete isolation and self-destruction. In November 1999, during an interview with *Rhythm* magazine, Chad Smith also opened up about his good friend overcoming his struggles and being back in the Red Hot Chili Peppers:

> John is a beautiful, talented and incredibly inspiring musician to me. There was a time when I thought he was going to die. He was immersed in a lifestyle that he had chosen, but for him – as a friend and a person that I care about – to be back among the living and playing music again was fantastic. It's something I never dreamed would happen.

Californication Red Hot Chili Peppers

To the delight of fans across the globe, Frusciante's return was revealed by way of a small show at the 9:30 Club in Washington, DC, on 12 June 1998. Two days later, the revitalised quartet played a short but triumphant set at the Tibetan Freedom Concert, which also took place in the nation's capital. The socio-political festival was first held in 1996, where money was raised for Tibetan and social justice causes. Later concerts were put on to help heighten awareness of the Tibetan Independence Movement as the province fought to break away from China's clutches. A Navarro-featuring Red Hot Chili Peppers performed on the second day of the 1996 event, but the band's set at the RFK Stadium two years later became a cornerstone moment for the group, even though, at one point, they weren't on the bill of performers.

The first day had been marred by severe storms, and a young girl was even struck by lightning. The remainder of the day's festivities were understandably cancelled, and to allow the likes of Radiohead and R.E.M. to come back and play on the Sunday, a handful of acts, including the Red Hot Chili Peppers, were removed from the lineup. Sunday's headliners were Pearl Jam, and their impassioned frontman, Eddie Vedder, took umbrage to the Chilis' omittance. With over 100,000 people in attendance, Vedder threatened to pull his band from the show if the Chilis weren't given an opportunity to play; he even went as far as to gift them 15 minutes of Pearl Jam's set time. And so the LA heroes took to the stage and played better than they had in almost six years. They only performed three songs that day, but not a second was wasted; a mesmerising rendition of 'Under The Bridge', which can still be viewed online today, captured the magic the band still had in them. The Red Hot Chili Peppers that people had been clamouring for were well and truly back and firing on all cylinders with renewed vigour and a fresh hunger in their bellies. A new road was pathed that day and it was a road that led straight to *Californication*.

Dreaming Of Californication

The Red Hot Chili Peppers spent much of the summer of 1998 writing and rehearsing in Flea's converted garage studio. New music was pouring out of the band, with Anthony Kiedis and John Frusciante experiencing a proficient bout of creativity. The quartet had recently aligned themselves with Q Prime Management, the revered company founded by Peter Mensch and Cliff Burnstein, who, at one point or another, would look after the careers of Metallica and the Smashing Pumpkins. After the Chilis played consecutive nights at the Aragon Ballroom in Chicago as part of Miller Genuine Draft's Blind Date Promotion – in which competition winners were given the chance to see big-name artists play in unusually intimate club settings – the band were then booked on a small late-summer tour. Q Prime's objective was to remind people that the Red Hot Chili Peppers were still very much alive and active.

By now, the nu metal movement was gaining strong mainstream attention, and it was the 'in thing' in alternative music. Amalgamating various styles of both hard rock and heavy metal and often including elements of funk and hip-hop, the Red Hot Chili Peppers were just one of many bands who were cited as a major influence on the burgeoning scene. Nu metal secured its first number-one album in the first week of September 1998 when Korn roared to the top of the *Billboard* 200 with their *Follow The Leader* album. Also released on the same day as Korn's third opus was Orgy's debut blend of industrial synth-rock, *Candyass*, which would go platinum thanks in no small part to their energetic cover of New Order's 'Blue Monday'. And the third of three big-hitting albums to drop on 18 August 1998 was Kid Rock's *Devil Without A Cause*. The rap rocker predicted that his breakthrough LP would go platinum in the States, and it did – and then again ten times more. Deftones, Limp Bizkit and Soulfly had also laid some solid foundations by this time, and in 1999, the floodgates fully opened. Much like how grunge had killed off hair metal, nu metal officially put paid to an early 1990s movement that seemingly waned at the exact moment the media announced Kurt Cobain's shocking suicide.

Alt rock was able to persevere, though, and as the world prepared itself for the new millennium, the Red Hot Chili Peppers remained the subgenre's greatest hope. Whether or not they were worried or even bothered about a possible decline in popularity, the four-piece didn't let it show in the material they were preparing for album number seven. With John Frusciante back in the fold, the Chilis returned to their melody-based songwriting. The guitarist, however, would take a more minimalistic approach on this occasion. When needed, the band were still able to rock with the best of them, and *Californication* would contain some absolute bangers. What instantly stood out upon first listening was the quality of the songs and the diversity of the sounds and styles to have been experimented with.

Interestingly, the band's initial idea was to move into an electronic direction, and with that in mind, they approached Brian Eno and William Orbit – both of whom were considered pioneers of ambient and electronic music – to potentially produce the record. David Bowie was also on the shortlist. *Blood Sugar Sex Magik* and *One Hot Minute* had both been produced by record label exec-turned-mega-impresario Rick Rubin, but the Chili Peppers were looking to move on and work with someone new this time around. However, none of the names on their shortlist were available, so they next turned to Daniel Lanois, who was greatly in demand after producing U2's classic trio of albums: *The Unforgettable Fire*, *The Joshua Tree* and *Achtung Baby*. Lanois was also unable to commit to the Chilis, having been put on a retainer by the Irish rockers, who were getting ready to begin work on what would become the hugely successful *All That You Can't Leave Behind*. To soften the blow somewhat, Lanois invited the quartet to use his Teatro studio to record some demos. In 2014, the sessions leaked online, and 15 years after the release of *Californication*, people were given the opportunity to go back and hear how the songs sounded in their infancy. The leak also revealed seven tracks that had never been heard before and likely never made it past the demo stage. These will be discussed later in this book.

At the time, Daniel Lanois was so impressed by what the Chilis had come up with when he played the tracks back that, regardless of his allegiance to U2, he offered to produce the then-untitled *Californication*, but the band had already reconnected with Rick Rubin. In December 1998, they entered Cello Studios to begin the album's recording. Located at 6000 West Sunset Boulevard and previously known as Western Recorders, Cello had only been in operation for a matter of months when the Red Hot Chili Peppers rolled up with Rubin in tow. Cello was renowned for its stellar-sounding live rooms and its plethora of vintage analogue equipment, including highly sought-after microphones and two custom-built Neve consoles. The band holed themselves up in Studio 2, a medium-sized room that was rectangular in shape, which helped generate a tight and punchy sound. To capture the spirit and vibrancy of their playing, all four members were recorded at the very same time. Chad Smith's drums sat on a riser in the middle of the room, Anthony Kiedis was just metres away in his vocal booth, while Frusciante and Flea completed a fine-tuned working circle with their amps situated in an isolation booth to prevent any leakage. The basic mic setup helped to create the big sound you hear on the album, especially the drumming, where mics were positioned next to each part of Smith's expansive kit. Recorded almost entirely in mono, there were very few effects and little to no reverb added later on, although there were some minor overdubs incorporated here and there. In an interview with music technology magazine *Sound On Sound* in December 1999, Jim Scott discussed engineering and mixing *Californication* and how everything recorded was 'already on point'. His main job involved balancing the tracks and working out where they had to sound louder and more intense. Scott also gave extremely high praise to the album's true masterminds:

> These guys are such great players. I have seen them go through highs and lows, but right now, they're really good. I think they are the best band around at the moment. The dedication of the band to get this record the best they could was awesome.

Further recording and mixing took place at The Village, previously a Masonic temple at 1616 Butler Avenue in West LA. Converted into a recording studio complex in 1968, the Red Hot Chili Peppers followed in the footsteps of The Rolling Stones, Fleetwood Mac and Eric Clapton by acclimatising themselves to Studio A. For additional keyboard parts, Greg Kurstin was brought in to contribute to a handful of tracks. An LA native, the multi-instrumentalist, songwriter and producer has since gone on to win nine Grammys, having worked with artists including the Foo Fighters and Adele. For a shorter guest spot, the Chilis also called in Patrick Warren, who has long been considered the world's best Chamberlin artist. A precursor to the Mellotron and first introduced in 1948, the Chamberlin organ is a kind of electro-mechanical keyboard. Warren's performance of the instrument can be heard in the album's closing track, 'Road Trippin".

Californication took a little over a month to record, followed by a few weeks of mixing. Fans were unaware at the time but the album was to present a stark departure from those that came before it. From the very first listen, you can feel the trauma of the band

Californication Red Hot Chili Peppers

members' life experiences, relayed through sombre melodies and introspective lyricism. With those experiences also came a newfound freedom and appreciation, knowing that, in Kiedis and Frusciante's cases in particular, they were still around to tell their tales. With time came healing; this was an overly mature rebirth of the Red Hot Chili Peppers.

If there were certain portions of their following who longed for a return to the funk-punk of the 1980s, where the band's naïve adolescence bore songs by the names of 'True Men Kill Coyotes' and 'Catholic School Girls Rule', it was abundantly clear from the opening tones of the album's lead single that *Californication* wasn't going to be for them. Instead, there is a clarity and dedication to the music in which the band make the most of the second chance afforded to them. A far more professional force than before, all four members were continually showing up to the studio on time, always in high spirits. Rick Rubin later commented on how the recording process was far more stress-free in comparison to the making of *One Hot Minute*, which was made during 'day-long pot sessions or sexual indulgences.' *Californication* wasn't going to suffer a similar fate.

Kiedis did endure a minor relapse prior to going into Cello Studios, but his bandmates stood by him to support rather than judge. The frontman spent some time living with Flea, where he renegotiated his focus and wrote what would become some of his finest-ever lyrics. Kiedis also took it upon himself to get some vocal training with Ron Anderson, whose long list of students has included Ozzy Osbourne, Axl Rose, Lenny Kravitz and Janet Jackson. The two worked together every day during recording, and the higher tones, tender harmonies and overall better singing Kiedis displays across the album's 56-minute running time shows just how far he had come in his recovery. In his *Scar Tissue* memoir, Kiedis perfectly summed up the band's feelings on what they had achieved with *Californication*:

> We were all thrilled when we finished work on the album. We felt like a forest that had burned to the ground and then new trees had sprouted from the ashes.

From the colourful and chaotic graffiti that promoted their debut in 1984 to the topless model (Dawn Alane) cradling the four miniaturised members of the band's 1989 lineup on *Mother's Milk*, or even Julian

Californication Red Hot Chili Peppers

Schnabel's vivid painting of his daughter and John Frusciante's then-girlfriend Stella on *By The Way*, the Red Hot Chili Peppers's album covers have always been intriguing from an artistic viewpoint. For *Californication*, the image depicted on the front cover is perhaps the most iconic of all of them despite its relative simplicity by comparison. It does, however, befit the themes of its title track in particular and the mindset that the quartet were in at the time.

California is known for many things, including the surrounding Pacific Ocean and scorching skies, but in keeping with the inverted ideals documented on *Californication*, its cover portrays a swimming pool full of flaming red and a sky made up of deep blue water. The whole idea came from a dream of John Frusciante's, and after sharing it with his bandmates, everyone was on board with wanting to bring the reverie to life. Anthony Kiedis drew up a very rough sketch and then he passed it on to Lawrence Azerrad, a designer who worked for Warner Bros. Records. In 2018, Azerrad won a Grammy for his work on the packaging of the *Voyager Golden Records 40th Anniversary Edition* before winning a second award in the same category three years later for his input on Wilco's *Ode To Joy* album.

Unlike today, where image creation and editing can be done on your mobile phone, in 1999, there was no such way of using stock photos to build a starting point. Instead, Azerrad, his team and the Red Hot Chili Peppers went out and searched for the perfect location and the perfect swimming pool. They took photos of those that they 'auditioned' and recorded them all in a physical portfolio. The pool that would earn the honour of featuring on the *Californication* cover – snapped by Sonia Koskoff – turned out to be owned by the parents of one of Azerrad's childhood friends. With the treetops and bushes that can be seen bordering the edge of the pool, it is believed its location was somewhere in the Hollywood Hills.

With everything now in place, Azerrad created a mock cover, exhausting all the limitations of a Photoshop program that was very much still a work in progress back then. He wanted the artwork to resemble that of a classic rock record, and after he replaced the sky with water and vice versa, he chose a small and simple text font to present the Red Hot Chili Peppers' name and the album title. The mock was as much as Azerrad could do, so his image was handed over to a set of designers who specialised in creating movie posters, and who had better technology at their disposal to make greater colour and resolution enhancements. The results revealed a cover equally as scenic as the light and reflective music that is displayed across the album, while its powerful transposition of colours represented the deeper songs that explored more jarring themes. With the final piece of the puzzle completed, *Californication* was ready to be unleashed on the world on 8 June 1999.

Californication

Personnel:
Anthony Kiedis: lead vocals
John Frusciante: lead electric and acoustic guitars, backing vocals, keyboards
Flea: electric and acoustic bass guitar, backing vocals
Chad Smith: drums
Greg Kurstin: additional keyboards
Patrick Warren: Chamberlin organ
Recorded at Cello Studios, Los Angeles, California (December 1998-March 1999)
Produced by: Rick Rubin
Record label: Warner Bros.
Release date: 8 June 1999
Chart positions: US: 3, UK: 5, AUS: 1
Running time: 56:24
All tracks written by the Red Hot Chili Peppers, unless otherwise stated

> I listened to it (*Californication*) the other day and I thought, 'Wow, it really is a pretty relaxed record.' And considering what we've been through, I would have thought it would be more edgy or something. I know for myself, a lot of times when we were recording the record, I was feeling so much emotional pain – hot and cold flashes and stuff. But it really is relaxed.
> Flea, *Guitar World*, July 1999

'Around The World'

The Chilis are indeed Red Hot as *Californication* begins with the rousing 'Around The World'. Perfectly demonstrating their exploration of the quiet-loud dynamic, the track finds the band back to their cohesive best, with Flea's heavily distorted bass riff assuming the lead before John Frusciante's indelible guitar licks bring an element of the Chilis' classic funk sound. Frusciante would use a host of different guitars across the album, most notably of which his '62 Fender Stratocaster. When he returned to the Chilis, almost all of his guitars had either been sold, stolen or had perished in a fire, so Anthony Kiedis bought the '62 Strat from a local Guitar Center. The instrument would become synonymous with Frusciante, who used it extensively during the recording of *Californication* and for many future albums. On 'Around The World', Frusciante grapples with his beat-up Fender Jaguar, which gives the song its overly thick sound. He wrote the guitar parts alone, while Flea thought up his bass parts shortly after. Upon Frusciante revealing his ideas to his bandmates, Chad Smith was able to keep up on the hi-hat before going on to provide the muscle with some fractious drum blasts. The pulsating instrumental intro brings to mind the beginning of a jam session, where, in this instance, the Chilis are shaking off any remaining ring rust – this is the perfect way to signify their triumphant return.

The song also contains some subtle keyboard entries by Greg Kurstin, as well as an Omnichord in the chorus – played by Frusciante, Flea and Jim Scott. 'You just press one button and you hear a chord, but it took three of us to do it', said Frusciante in a *Guitar World* interview in July 1999, as he divulged how they had to slow down the tape for one chord and then speed it back up for the other chords that were being played.

'Around The World' documents Anthony Kiedis' experiences of life on the road, partly inspired by Roberto Benigni's 1997 comedy film *Life Is Beautiful* – of which Kiedis uses the title in his own vivid lyrical tales of the world he has so far travelled. The frontman confidently raps about 'The motherfuckin' girls of California' – the emphatic expletive ultimately preventing the song from being played on certain radio stations. Kiedis also mentions visiting Sicily, Bombay, the Swiss mountains and 'Living in and out of a big fat suitcase' on verses driven by Frusciante's simple but effective funk riff and Flea's deep finger-picked bass groove. The dedicated vocal training Kiedis undertook during the album's recording clearly paid off because much of his range is showcased in this song – from the fiery roar during the intro to the cleaner and melodic tones he expels throughout the swirling chorus. He even finds room for a scat vocal in the final hook, his 'Ding, dang, dong, dong, ding, ding, dong, dong, ding, dang' passage emerging from a brief period of writer's block. This extremely random bout of filler was later kept in at the request of Flea's daughter, Clara.

With an original working title of 'All Around The World', the album opener was chosen as the second single and released on CD and cassette in the UK on 23 August 1999, on CD in Japan on 8 September and to radio only in America on 28 September. The song peaked at 25 in the UK, while in the US, it reached number seven and 16 on *Billboard*'s Modern Rock Tracks and Mainstream Rock Tracks charts, respectively. An accompanying music video was directed by Frenchman Stéphane Sednaoui, whom the Red Hot Chili Peppers had previously worked with on the promos for 'Give It Away', 'Breaking The Girl' and 'Scar Tissue'. As he had with 'Give It Away', Sednaoui produced a similarly vibrant presentation for 'Around The World' revolving around a full-band performance. Utilising various camera and editing techniques, the results proved equally colourful and chaotic. The video isn't one of the Chilis' most memorable, but at a time when they presented themselves more seriously than in the past, the fact the four can be seen gyrating and acting aloof at regular intervals showed they were still having a lot of fun in the process.

In 2001, a heavily edited version of 'Around The World' was used to coincide with the launch of the California Screamin' rollercoaster at the Disneyland resort in Anaheim, and in 2010, the song was selected as the opening theme of *Beck* – a live-action film adaptation of the popular Japanese manga series. A year later, the so-called 'Big Four' record labels of EMI, Sony, Universal and Warner collaborated on a charity compilation album to help with relief efforts for those affected by the 3 March Tōhoku earthquake and tsunami, which led to the deaths of over 20,000 people. The album, simply titled *Songs For Japan*, featured 33 songs by 33 different artists, and along with the likes of John Lennon, Bob Dylan, U2 and Elton John, a live recording of 'Around The World' was chosen as the Red Hot Chili Peppers' contribution. Over 500,000 copies of the album have been sold to date, and over $5,000,000 has been raised towards the relief efforts.

'Around The World' has remained a constant in the band's live setlists ever since its debut and is a strong statement of intent from the Red Hot Chili Peppers. It may not be talked about with the same admiration as some of the other songs found on *Californication*, but if anything, this is the sound of a band that perhaps felt the need to remind everyone they were still around and still capable of creating brilliant rock songs. 'Around The World' is the first of many highlights to come.

'Parallel Universe'

Maintaining the album's up-tempo beginning, 'Parallel Universe' offers a first glimpse into Anthony Kiedis' new outlook on life. His lyrics are, at times, ambiguous, but they are extremely poetic and philosophical, with verses hinting at dream-like musings. Delivering spiritual lines ('You could die but you're never dead') and psychedelic turns ('Take a look at the stars in your head, fields of space kid'), Kiedis sounds a little subdued on this occasion, allowing John Frusciante and Flea to

Californication Red Hot Chili Peppers

dual behind him. Trading palm-muted notes over Chad Smith's persistent beat, 'Parallel Universe' follows a fairly simple formula for the majority of its existence until the chorus' heavily distorted guitar takes things up a notch. During the hook, Kiedis announces himself as both a 'Sidewinder' and a 'California king', both of which happen to be types of snakes. The former connotes danger and untrustworthiness, whilst the latter relates to his feeling of becoming one of California's most notorious musical exports. These are interesting references which undoubtedly stem from his period of personal reflection.

Simply known as 'Universe' in its early stages, the second track of an already promising *Californication* is notable for its exclusion of funk bass and backing vocals – something that is particularly unusual for a Red Hot Chili Peppers song. Instead, the quartet focus on raw power, as further underlined by the explosive burst of instrumentation that plays out the track. Frusciante's rabid guitar solo sounds like it is coming from a man who continues to cleanse his soul, supported by Flea and Smith's equally colourful but rhythmic assaults. Rarely have the Chilis sounded so urgent and heavy, and while it could have something to do with the album's harsh and rather dry mixing, it doesn't take away from how quickly 'Parallel Universe' became a fan favourite song.

The sixth and final single taken from *Californication* and released solely to radio on 24 March 2001, 'Parallel Universe' still made it to number 37 on the Modern Rock Tracks chart despite there being no physical copies pressed nor a music video filmed to promote it.

'Scar Tissue'

The legacy of *Blood Sugar Sex Magik* was partially built on the back of 'Under The Bridge' – a startlingly honest rock ballad where Anthony Kiedis revealed his struggles with trying to stay clean from heroin and the isolation he faced from being deep into addiction. It was a song the singer felt reluctant to share with his bandmates at first, but 'Under The Bridge' would prove to be a major breakthrough moment for the Red Hot Chili Peppers.

A few weeks before the release of *Californication*, the quartet unveiled the album's lead single, 'Scar Tissue', which, more than any other song, presented the band's new sound and style. Led by Frusciante's delicate and sombre guitar, this vulnerable song finds Kiedis once again reflecting on the harsh reality that he and other addicts go through during recovery. Having gone unnoticed by many over the years, including most of the band and even Rick

Californication Red Hot Chili Peppers

Rubin, the song's prominent guitar part has since been revealed to be out of tune. In 2019, YouTuber Paul Davids made a video in which he attempted to recreate the song's delectable intro, and after further inspection, he discovered that the only way to successfully moniker it was by detuning his guitar's B-string. Davids then questioned whether Frusciante had intentionally done the same, making the string flat to enhance the sound of the intervals. During an appearance on Rick Rubin's *Broken Record* podcast in December 2022, Frusciante finally revealed that his guitar was indeed out of tune, but only by accident:

> It wasn't done consciously – I was just out of tune. I guess one of my strings was a little out of tune and it sounded good, so nobody ever said anything.

Frusciante also spoke of likening the song's tuning to microtonal music, where additional notes are incorporated between those that usually appear in the common 12-note chromatic scale:

> You have notes (cents) in between the normal 12 notes that we all use, and there's a lot of good expression in there by using these notes that are in between – if they are exactly in between in a precise kind of way. So I guess I was out of tune in a way that really worked because that doesn't sound out of tune to me.

With its title referencing the naturality of the human healing process, the inspiration behind 'Scar Tissue' was never going to be too hard to decipher, but the way Kiedis details his journey demonstrated just how far he had come as a lyricist. The repetitive chorus line of 'With the birds I'll share this lonely viewin'' is the prime example of summoning relatability in his words, especially for those who have managed to turn their lives around.

Frusciante's atmospheric guitar effortlessly paints the song's overbearing mood, while Flea's minimalistic bassline and Chad Smith's measured beat find the song's true power coming from its sparseness. The cathartic and crowning glory comes via Frusciante's stunning slide guitar solos, which appear on either side of one last chorus refrain and allow the listener to experience multiple emotions during its exhibition. As uplifting as it is pained, the solo would become the one to put the Chilis in a whole new league of their own and one which all of Frusciante's future efforts would be measured against.

In Kiedis' memoir of the same name, he reminisced on how 'Scar Tissue' came together:

> When John started playing this guitar riff, I immediately knew what the song was about. It was a playful, happy-to-be-alive, phoenix-rising-from-the-ashes vibe. I ran outside with my handheld tape recorder and, with that music playing in the background, started singing the entire chorus of the song.

To accompany the single release, the Chilis went out to the Mojave Desert to film a music video. Directed by Stéphane Sednaoui, the scenic clip follows a bloodied and bruised Red Hot Chili Peppers as they drive along the highway in an equally beaten-up 1967 Pontiac convertible. All four members appear to be in a thoughtful state as they kick back and inhale the fresh desert air, seemingly preparing for their rebirth. Released on 25 May – just two weeks ahead of *Californication* – 'Scar Tissue' spent a then-record 16 consecutive weeks atop *Billboard*'s Hot Modern Rock Tracks chart. The song also hit number one on the Mainstream Rock and Alternative Airplay charts, as well as scoring a strong number nine placing on the Hot 100. 'Scar Tissue' would sell in excess of 4,000,000 copies in America and won a Grammy at the 2000 Awards for Best Rock Song.

Considered by fans and critics alike as one of their best-ever tracks, the Red Hot Chili Peppers really came out fighting on 'Scar Tissue'. With John Frusciante in tow, the band were fully reunited and they possessed a resilience and desire to never make the same mistakes again. The lead single off any album is usually considered to be the most important, and while it wasn't the bouncing rock anthem people may have been expecting, 'Scar Tissue' explored new territory for the Red Hot Chili Peppers, which ultimately and rather unexpectedly would lead them to even wider acclaim. 'Scar Tissue' may just be one of the last defining songs of the 1990s, and in the process, it became a certified classic.

'Otherside'
Effectively acting as a companion piece to 'Scar Tissue', Anthony Kiedis continues to confront the battles that addicts face in steering clear of temptation on the equally striking 'Otherside'. The song's title is uncharacteristically stylised as one word to partly reference the afterlife

This balladic, pure rock number provides further evidence of the Red Hot Chili Peppers' new approach to songwriting. During the album's promotion, the band discussed on more than one occasion how John Frusciante had to adapt his playing style for the new material. The guitarist was heavily into minimalism at the time, which certainly influenced his thought process during the writing sessions. He was, however, still dealing with the aftereffects of his own drug addictions, which had caused him to lose a degree of strength in his hands and fingers. *Californication* would still contain some of Frusciante's signature and intense guitar licks, as heard on 'Around The World' and 'Parallel Universe', for example, but there was now a move to shine a more linear focus on texture and melody.

Built around an intricate structure, 'Otherside' opens with a catchy little guitar ditty from Frusciante's Gretsch White Falcon, as Kiedis announces himself with a measured retort of the 'How long, how long will I slide?' chorus line – the singer openly revealing his expectation of an inevitable relapse. The guitar melodies hint at another Red Hot Chili Peppers classic-in-the-making, and musically, the verses remain sweet and solemn as the reserved bassline and softly tapped drums play second fiddle to Frusciante's spinetingling tones. All the while, Kiedis delivers one of his strongest performances with a vocal containing another burst of lyrics that are shrouded in metaphors. There is even an apparent nod in the direction of Hillel Slovak – the Chilis' original guitarist, who himself lost his fight with addiction. The mournful line, 'I heard your voice through a photograph, I thought it up and brought up the past', adds even greater weight to the song's overall meaning. As 'Otherside' progresses, so does the intensity, and with the song building towards its absorbing finale, the line of 'I yell and tell it that it's not my friend, I tear it down, I tear it down, and then it's born again' is quite frankly one of the most heartbreaking and honest lyrics Kiedis could have written on such subject matter. Kiedis' *Scar Tissue* memoir was still some years away from coming to fruition at this point, and so *Californication* was the first time he had so frequently chosen to bare his soul to the world.

Allowing the symbolism of the lyrics a visual platform, a music video was filmed to accompany the release of 'Otherside' as the album's third single. The Chilis enlisted Jonathan Dayton and Valerie Faris – the husband-and-wife director duo who, throughout the 1990s, had cut their teeth by working with R.E.M., Extreme and the Smashing Pumpkins. Influenced by German expressionist art and the

Californication Red Hot Chili Peppers

20th-century Cubism movement, the video presented gothic sensibilities through its largely black and white/monochrome colour scheme. Following a cartoon-like narrative and interspersed with shots of the band, the main theme of the video explores a young man's nightmare, in which he battles various demons that are perceived to be himself. Ultimately, he ends up being back in the very same place where he began, and thus, the plot alludes to addiction and the vicious and repetitive cycle a user finds themselves immersed in.

Also featuring some typically stirring backing vocals, a passionate guitar solo and a chorus simply made for the radio airwaves, it was no surprise that 'Otherside' was chosen for a single release. Arriving in Australia, New Zealand and Japan in December 1999, and then in the US and UK during January 2000, the song's main success predictably came in the Chilis' homeland. 'Otherside' made it to number 14 on the Hot 100 and number one on the Alternative Airplay chart, where it stayed for 14 straight weeks. The single also sold over 3,000,000 copies and, therefore, achieved triple platinum status.

'Get On Top'

With *Californication* seemingly settling into a serious flow, the Red Hot Chili Peppers now throw a spanner in the works by next unleashing the boisterous 'Get On Top'. Upon the instant arrival of John Frusciante's wah-infused guitar, the song feels like it is coming straight out of the *Blood Sugar Sex Magik* playbook – or any of the band's albums to come before *Californication*, for that matter. The instrumentation and lyricism exude power and a degree of rebellion. The track was devised in a jam session where Frusciante unmasked a swaggering rhythm inspired by hip-hop icons Public Enemy, who he had listened to earlier in the day. 'Get On Top' somewhat follows the rap rock formula with its energetic bounce, its wiry bass thump and emphatic drumbeat. Kiedis spits venom on the mic, as he uses skilful wordplay surrounding a desire for control and dominance. 'Come with me 'cause I'm an ass killer, you're ill but I'm iller' reeks of confidence – arrogance even – before the frontman speaks of lingering on blocks and giving the middle finger to cops. There is even a defiant C-bomb thrown in for good measure – not because it sounds cool, but simply because Kiedis wanted to.

The song's furious funk element is down to Frusciante once again, who liked to use Flea's Ibanez WH-10 Wah pedal for its big tone and wide range. Although the pedal had separate switches for bass and guitar, it was actually the bass setting Frusciante chose to use here to effectively capture his furious playing style. There is also a rather subtle solo thrown into the middle of the track, which suits the overall rhythm. Inspired by the guitarist's love of the progressive rock band Yes, who laid down a similar sounding solo on their 1972 song 'Siberian Khatru', Frusciante was intent on adding something that he later remarked would 'create a contrast between the solo and the background'. Its inclusion only strengthens the song's funkiness and drive that refuses to subside across its 3:18 running time.

In February 2001, 'Get On Top' was featured in an episode of the HBO prison drama *Oz* (season four, episode 16). In 2005, the song was supposed to be included on the soundtrack of the *Herbie Fully Loaded* movie, but for reasons unknown, it was inexplicably replaced by Aly and AJ's cover of 'Walking On Sunshine'. Two years later, 'Get On Top' was used as the backing music in the first trailer to promote Sony Pictures' new animated movie, *Surf's Up*.

Following such iconic songs as 'Scar Tissue' and 'Otherside' was always going to be a difficult task, but 'Get On Top' offers some brief respite from the bleak (but brilliant) state that the album appeared to be settling into. If anything, it showed fans that the Chilis were still capable of launching into relentless funk rock bangers whenever they felt like it, and despite them appearing to have come of age, the quartet still had some antagonistic verve should they wish to reveal it.

'Californication'

Before we've even reached the midway point comes the epic and masterful centrepiece of the entire album.

In an interview with *Q* magazine in July 1999, and at a time when some were still searching for the meaning behind the 'Californication' term, Anthony Kiedis touched on 'The beautiful and ugly effects' that California had spread on the rest of the world. He extended on this, and the title track, with Italian publication *Hard!* in the same month when he called the song 'Our love-n-hatred ballad' – he certainly got the hatred part right. Behind its picturesque finger-picked guitar chords, infectious bass notes and a military-style drumbeat comes a scathing exposé on the Golden State and, in particular, Hollywood, the band spurred on by having witnessed first-hand the toxic allure that shrouds the city.

'Californication' is considered by many as Kiedis' greatest work, his thoughts and feelings shining through lyrical poetry as he attacks the

Californication Red Hot Chili Peppers

superficiality that he links to the deterioration of society. Kiedis wrote most of the song's lyrics during what he called a 'cleansing trip' to Thailand, with certain lines stemming from his own experiences with people around him. In his *Scar Tissue* memoir, he wrote of 'coming across a crazy lady on the street, ranting about the fact that there were psychic spies in China'. That memory would help formulate the song's opening line of 'Psychic spies from China try to steal your mind's elation'. Tinged with tragedy, 'A teenage bride with a baby inside getting high on information' was born out of a therapy meeting Kiedis attended, where he met a young mother who was losing her battle with sobriety. That same character would get her own song on the album a little later, but these are just two moments that, like every line, strike a nerve with all who are listening.

Deadly arrows are aimed in the direction of those seeking fame and fortune ('Little girls from Sweden dream of silver screen quotations/Buy me a star on the boulevard') and there are unmasked attacks on people obsessed with plastic surgery ('Pay your surgeon very well to break the spell of aging'). Mentions of Kurt Cobain and David Bowie's *Station To Station* album reference pop culture and offer a momentary break in the doom and gloom, but it isn't long before the frontman's tirade gains a second wind.

Kiedis had clearly taken note of how, even as far out as Asia, American culture had manifested itself into global territories, and as he wrote his lyrics, he was also thinking up some melody structures. Those parts came together before there had been any talk of John Frusciante's return to the band, and while the guitarist was able to slot back in nicely, 'Californication' became something of a problem song for the Red Hot Chili Peppers. 'For some reason, even though there was a perfect song in there, we couldn't find it', Kiedis wrote in his memoir. 'All these other songs were pouring out of us', he continued. 'We'd been working for a few weeks when someone started playing an ultra-sparse riff that sounded like nothing we'd ever done before. As soon as I heard it, I knew it was our new song.'

With some of the song's early obstacles overcome, another reared its head when Flea, Smith and even Frusciante expressed a lack of desire to record 'Californication', feeling they already had more than enough material to make up the album. Kiedis fought like hell for his song to be heard, and even in its early stages, he was adamant it would become 'The anchor of the whole record'. His bandmates finally relented, and after only rehearsing the song twice, they went into the studio and recorded it.

Above: LA's finest foursome in 1999. (*Tony Woolliscroft*)

Californication Red Hot Chili Peppers

Left: Dreaming of ... the iconic album cover art. (*Warner Bros*)

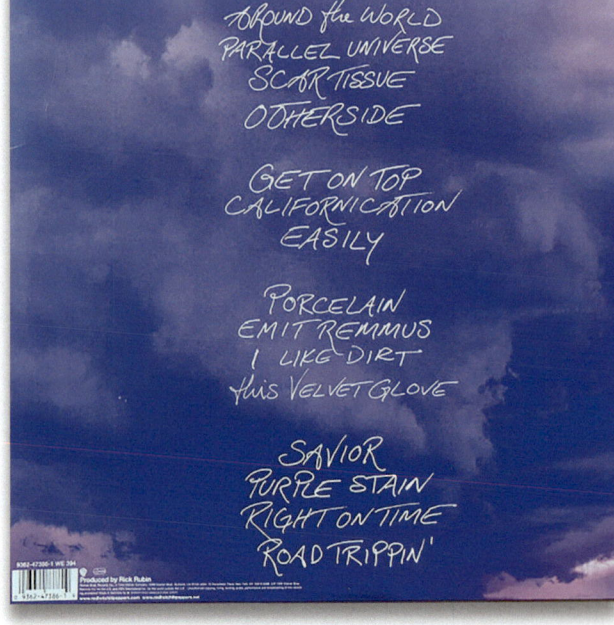

Right: The rear cover art: simple but effective. (*Warner Bros*)

Californication Red Hot Chili Peppers

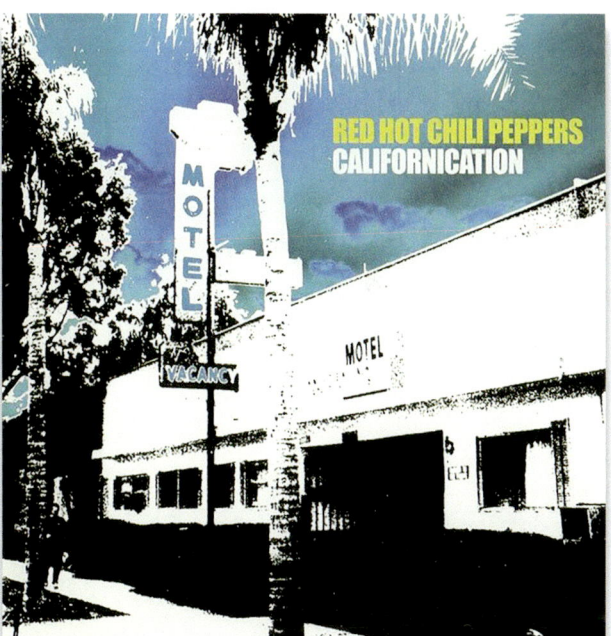

Right: The 'Californication' single cover art. (*Warner Bros*)

Left: A rather stormy cover for the 'Otherside' single. (*Warner Bros*)

Californication Red Hot Chili Peppers

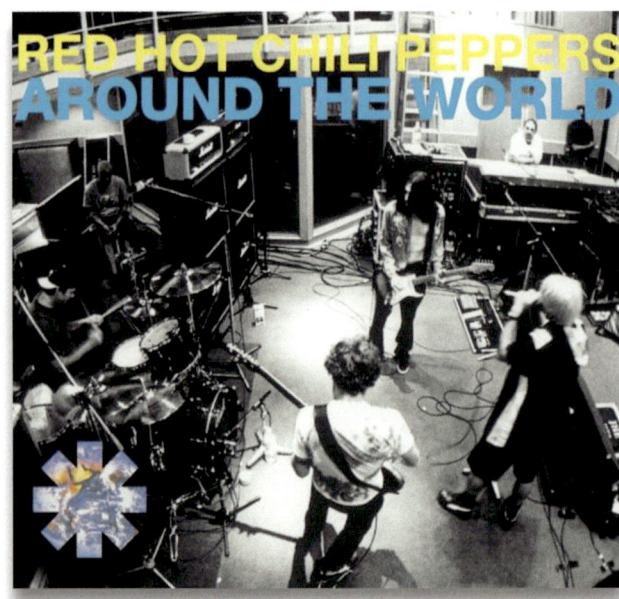

Left: All Around the … studio. The album's hard-rocking second single. (*Warner Bros*)

Right: The final official single, 'Road Trippin' became a huge fan favourite in next to no time. (*Warner Bros*)

Californication Red Hot Chili Peppers

Above: A still from the enthralling 'Californication' music video.

Below: A beaten but unbroken Anthony Kiedis on the set of the 'Scar Tissue' music video.

Californication Red Hot Chili Peppers

Above: Just chillin' – a video still from 'Road Trippin''.

Below: Symbolism was key in the 'Otherside' video.

Californication Red Hot Chili Peppers

Above: Kiedis, Flea and John Frusciante rocking out at the *Billboard* Awards in 1999. (*Scott Gries*)

Right: The *Californication* world tour included a stop at the historic Wembley Arena.

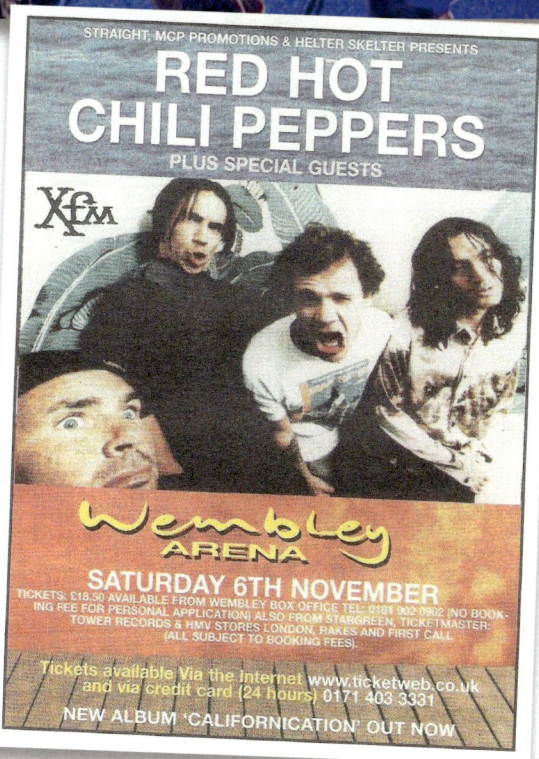

Californication Red Hot Chili Peppers

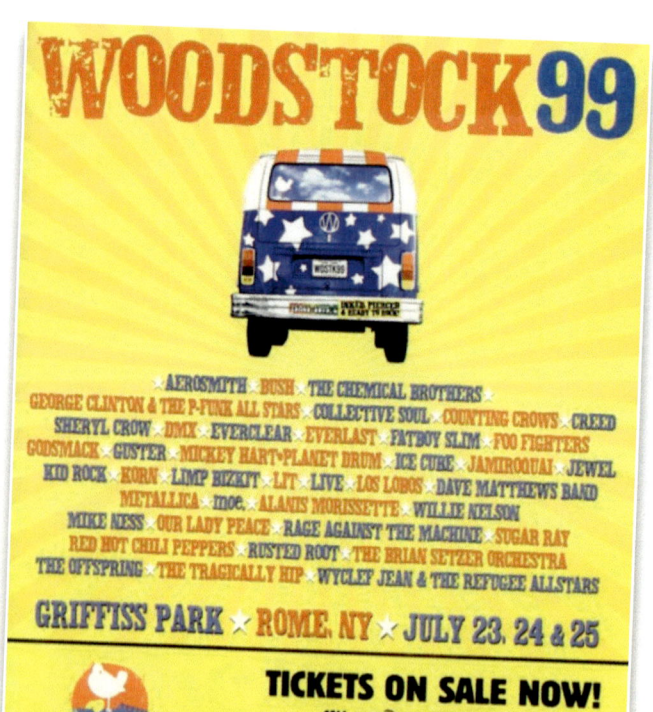

Left: A promotional poster for what would become the most infamous festival in music history.

Above: The Chilis headlining Woodstock '99. Thankfully, a completely naked Flea wasn't facing the camera at this moment.

Clocking in at 5:21, 'Californication' became an instant hit with fans, who applauded the band's ability to create a yin-yang effect where such heavy subject matter was presented through tender and delectable musicianship. Even its chorus, made up of a conservative and repeated three-word battle cry ('Dream of Californication'), sounds catchier than a fever, its understated impact enhancing the song's appeal even further.

Another perfect single option, 'Californication' was the album's fourth, released in June 2000. Topping the Alternative Airplay and Mainstream Rock charts was hardly surprising, while a number 69 placing on the Hot 100 wasn't to be sniffed at either. The single sold over 5,000,000 copies in the US and over 1,200,000 in the UK, where it also peaked at number 16 on the nation's chart. As good as the song 'Californication' was, these results were strong considering it, along with the rest of the album, had been digested for over a year by now, but the power of radio had done its job and continued to push the Red Hot Chili Peppers further into the mainstream eye.

A portion of the song's success has to be down to its brilliant music video, which was once again directed by Jonathan Dayton and Valerie Faris. Starring the Chilis as characters in their own open-world video game, each member runs, jumps, surfs or flies around various parts of California. Flea is seen running along Hollywood's Walk of Fame, Chad Smith goes snowboarding down Mammoth Mountains and Kiedis goes swimming with sharks and a host of bikini-clad ladies. As well as moments in scenes relating to certain song lyrics, there are further depictions of California with visual references to bear hunting, deforestation and porn sets, all the while a timer in the corner of the screen counts down to zero. As the quartet race towards downtown Los Angeles, ducking and diving out of the way of crashing vehicles and falling buildings, it is revealed that an earthquake is about to destroy the city.

The symbolism of the ending is rather obvious and draws parallels to another line in the song – 'Tidal waves couldn't save the world from Californication'. Whether intentional or not, this seems to align with the thoughts of another notable celebrity – comedian and satirist Bill Hicks, who also shared a hatred for the West Coast state. Hicks was known for his uncensored views on a wide range of social issues and he frequently used dark humour to get his points across. One of Hicks' most famous pieces is known as 'Arizona Bay', where he speaks of his hope that Los Angeles would one day fall into the ocean after suffering a cataclysmic earthquake.

Californication Red Hot Chili Peppers

He never hid his idea that the world would be a better place if LA wasn't part of it, and during one of his performances, he discernibly envisaged the event:

> All the shitty shows are gone, all the idiots screaming in the fucking wind are dead, I love it. Leaving nothing but a cool, beautiful serenity called … Arizona Bay … when LA falls into the fucking ocean and is flushed away, all that it will leave … is Arizona Bay.

The progressive metal band Tool referenced Hicks' same speech in their 1996 track 'Ænema', while British rockers Radiohead dedicated their 1994 album *The Bends* to Hicks, so it is highly plausible that Anthony Kiedis could have also tipped his hat to the comedian in this instance.

The 'Californication' video is by far the Red Hot Chili Peppers' most watched on YouTube, where today it has amassed over one billion views on the platform. At the MTV VMAs in 2000, the video was nominated for five awards, and although it lost out in the Video of the Year, Best Group Video and Best Special Effects categories, 'Californication' won the Best Direction and Best Art Direction prizes. At the same ceremony, the Red Hot Chili Peppers won the Video Vanguard Award, also known as the Lifetime Achievement Award, which is issued to an artist for outstanding contributions and profound impact on music videos and popular culture.

In 2022, Spanish developer and avid Chili Peppers fan Miquel Camps Orteza released a playable game based on the 'Californication' music video. Made downloadable to users of Windows and Mac computers, the game featured seven levels that were based on scenes you see in the promo clip. Whether the band welcomed the game or not, you have to praise Orteza's attention to detail that went into giving fans like himself the opportunity to immerse themselves into the world of 'Californication'.

Just as infectious as the location is for many who long to visit the West Coast, 'Californication' is an eye-opening meditation on the underbelly of what is seen to be the place where dreams are made. It is a song that will forever remain poignant and painfully honest, and even though it didn't win a Grammy at the 2001 awards (nominated for Best Rock Performance and Best Rock Song), just to be acknowledged underlined how deep the song had penetrated the public's psyche. It is undoubtedly one of the Red Hot Chili Peppers' best-ever songs.

'Easily'

Bookending 'Californication' with two uptempo rockers, 'Easily' comes in with a stylish riff and a pulsing drumbeat. This is the Red Hot Chili Peppers at their uncompromising best, and although 'Easily' is comparatively different from 'Get On Top', both rely on the same funk undercurrent that had served the band so well throughout the career up to this point.

Revealing one of Kiedis' most confident vocal performances on the entire album, and with a degree of swagger to boot, the singer relays another set of intriguingly deep lyrics. For some, they could have been considered part love story ('Let's get carried away/let's get married today'), while for others, they appear to communicate some kind of longing for world peace ('The story of a woman on the morning of a war/remind me if you will exactly what we're fighting for'), but as Kiedis goes on, it seems he may actually be searching for his own inner peace. During the rousing chorus, his defiant sequence of 'Throw me to the wolves because there's order in the pack/throw me to the sky because I know I'm coming back' shows his new and apparently positive mindset, where in order to find true value and self-worth, he is willing to let go of his ego and materialistic possessions.

The arcane lyrics are juxtaposed with instrumentation that is slightly more simplified on this occasion. Frusciante's layered guitar work reinforces the song's funk foundations through both tone and tuning. His two high-pitched solos, which come halfway through and then during a rousing outro, are highlights as Frusciante continues to sound like he is on the form of his life. Chad Smith contributes one of his best drumming performances, too, thrashing and pounding his kit with resounding force. At times, he dominates, and all the while, he controls the song's surging tempo.

'Easily' could, quite easily, have been a contender for a single release, but with so many outstanding songs to choose from, this one quickly settled into its role of being a very strong album track.

'Porcelain'

On 'Porcelain', Anthony Kiedis extends on his encounter with a young mother and addict at a Los Angeles YWCA, having previously found inspiration from her desperate plight to pen the 'Teenage bride with a baby inside…' line on 'Californication'. In his *Scar Tissue* memoir, Kiedis magnificently wrote how 'The beauty and sadness and tragedy and glory – all wrapped into one – of this mother/

daughter relationship was evoked by the vibe of that music', and the vibe in question would reveal yet another new side of the Red Hot Chili Peppers.

'Porcelain' is a slow and sauntering number, funereal even, and in some ways, it resembles a mid-album interlude instead of an actual song. With flourishes of 1960s psychedelic rock through gently picked, hazy guitar and bass, the spotlight is left to Kiedis – the master storyteller. His tender vocals are shrouded in a hopeless depression, reeking of fragility – much akin to porcelain dolls themselves. Alluding to perfect exteriors and hollow insides, the impact that the young mother's situation had on Kiedis is revealed in the standout lyric: 'Are you wasting away in your skin?/Are you missing the love of your kin?/Drifting and floating and fading away'. It's as beautiful as it is heart-wrenching.

In and out in less than three minutes and coming across as if it may have even been recorded live, the austere 'Porcelain' surprised a lot of people with just how different the song sounded in comparison to everything else the Red Hot Chili Peppers had written over the years. Some loved it and some regarded the song as a bit of a throwaway. What was clear, however, was how this new and ruminative era of the Chilis was always going to throw a curveball or two into the mix, and 'Porcelain' was a sumptuous curveball, to say the least.

'Emit Remmus'

Telling the story of a Transatlantic summer romance, 'Emit Remmus' is partly inspired by, of all people, Melanie Chisholm from the Spice Girls. Anthony Kiedis joined Flea and the bassist's daughter, Clara, in attending one of the British girl group's concerts on their *Spiceworld* tour in August 1998, which is when the frontman met the more commonly known Mel C backstage. The pair would hit it off and spend time together in LA, getting tattoos and simply enjoying one another's company. Various media outlets have since spoken of them as former partners. However, Kiedis and Chisholm have never hinted at their relationship being anything more than strictly platonic. Either way, 'Sporty Spice' clearly left enough of an impression on Kiedis that he would write a song that was loosely based on their time together.

'Emit Remmus' is, of course, 'summer time' spelt backwards and possibly signifies how opposite the London and LA summers are. It could also relate to the fact that the song's guitar parts were recorded in reverse. Over piercing guitar drones, Flea's bobbing bassline and Chad Smith's elevated drum fills, Kiedis sings of walking through

Leicester Square and up and down Primrose Hill before asking, 'What could be wetter than an English girl, American man'.

Unequivocally Red Hot Chili Peppers in both sound and style, the verses again give off a jam session vibe, especially with the experimental guitar work. The band then ramp up the power for a strong chorus, where Frusciante is in full shredding mode as he attempts to overthrow Smith's mighty drum rhythms. This is one of the heavier compositions on *Californication*, especially during its thunderous hook, but 'Emit Remmus' does lack the impetus showcased on the record's other tracks. It is also the song that, more than any other, suffers from the rough mixing that has plagued the legacy of *Californication* since its release (to be discussed later). Overall, this is a deep cut that, like 'Porcelain', has consistently divided opinion.

'I Like Dirt'

The super funky 'I Like Dirt' is a less than three-minute romp where Anthony Kiedis' rapping is littered with sexual innuendo. 'Live to love and give good tongue', 'Some come slow and overload' and 'Let's unzip and let's unfold' need no further deciphering as the lyrics are spouted over Flea's signature bass funk, Smith's unadulterated grooves and Frusciante's determined, finger-picked riffing.

The Red Hot Chili Peppers briefly return to their old ways here, even if their less serious and tongue-in-cheek antics feel a little out of place on an album that, until now, has emphasised such fervent maturity. The quartet undoubtedly sound tight and their playing is extremely cohesive, but it was always going to be difficult to replicate the quality of the stacked first side of *Californication*, which could be argued is near-perfect and full of classics.

Frusciante's raucous, blues-tinged solo on the final stretch supplies the most memorable moment, cementing 'I Like Dirt' as a playfully catchy and mischievous number.

'This Velvet Glove'

In 1998, Anthony Kiedis met Yohanna Logan in a New York restaurant – it was love at first sight. Logan was an addict, but Kiedis stood by her anyway, and when she chose to kick her habit and pursue her dream of becoming a fashion designer, the Red Hot Chili Peppers frontman helped finance her studies at the New York Fashion Institute. Kiedis, who described Logan as his soulmate, wrote in his *Scar Tissue* memoir that she was 'Probably the girl I loved the most

Californication Red Hot Chili Peppers

of all my girlfriends, but also the toughest one to make things work out with.' Needless to say, the relationship was on-off from the beginning. The couple finally called it quits in 2002 when Kiedis reportedly wanted to start a family, but Logan was too busy with her thriving label, *Shawn*, which Kiedis had helped set up, model outfits for and source contacts to bring the brand greater exposure.

'This Velvet Glove' is an honest and emotional love letter to Yohanna Logan, where Kiedis' lyrics describe the exultation of overcoming addiction and learning to enjoy life again. His wordplay is exceptional here, none more so than on the tongue-twisting 'It's such a waste to be wasted in the first place/I want to taste the taste of being face-to-face with common grace'. The song is atmospheric and upbeat, centred around John Frusciante's understated melodies. His acoustic guitar lead drives things forward, but it's the glossy electric riff layered on top which gives the track its charm and personality.

Twice does Kiedis declare, 'I'd take a fall and you know that I'd do anything I will for you', with gentle caution evident in his voice. Much like the meaning behind the song's title – drawn from Napoleon Bonaparte's famous 'iron fist in a velvet glove' metaphor – Kiedis is right to feel trepidation in a relationship that was anything but plain sailing, but listening to 'This Velvet Glove' and imagining him wearing pair of rose-tinted glasses, it seemed clear that, in 1999, love conquered all.

The frontman found further inspiration from a song Frusciante had been working on for one of his solo projects, describing in a *Juice Magazine* interview in December 1999 how he lifted a line from it to birth the 'John says to live above hell and my will is well' lyric. In the same interview, Kiedis spoke of 'This Velvet Glove' also being a tribute to his guitar player and brother-in-arms:

> He was singing about living life above hell, meaning whether from drugs or just a state of mind. He'd sampled life living in hell; he thought better of it, got over it and was living in a more beautiful space. I was so deeply in love when I wrote it, and John was very much a part of my life during that time, creating good energy, (and) I wanted to mention it.

In a 2001 chat with *Rockaxis.com*, Frusciante revealed 'This Velvet Glove' to be his favourite track on *Californication*, and it does indeed feature some of his best work: the electric melodies beautifully swaying over the acoustic lead and the contrasting tones evoking feelings of warmth and perseverance.

Largely unheralded at first due to the focus on the album's big hitters, 'This Velvet Glove' would become a big fan favourite in later years. The song is an addictive exploration of funk-infused rock and another that concentrates on the theme of overcoming the odds and being around to tell the story. This triumphant cut was ultimately inspired by the best medicine of all – love.

'Savior'

In 1974, 12-year-old Anthony Kiedis left Michigan and his mother to go and live with his father in Los Angeles. Kiedis' idyllic vision of becoming an adopted Californian seemed as much a fairytale as Hollywood itself in the early stages, but like many who came to the city before and after him would find out, his illusions of grandeur would soon be shattered.

John Michael Kiedis, AKA Blackie Dammett, dreamed of becoming an actor, but in the meantime, he got by as a drug dealer. Father and son relationships are often forged through watching or playing sports together, working on cars together or going fishing together, and young Anthony idolised his daddy. But in return, Blackie exposed his son to drink, drugs, wild parties and sex. Anthony would soon become accustomed to cocaine and marijuana, and when he was just 14, he experienced heroin for the first time when he snorted a line of what he thought was cocaine. Perhaps most alarming of all, and with Anthony yet to enter his teenage years, he would lose his virginity to Blackie's 18-year-old girlfriend when he was just 12. The 'deal', as Kiedis called it, was even 'brokered' by his father. We all know that Anthony would go on to enjoy a successful career as part of one of modern rock's biggest bands, but he was destined to suffer from his upbringing at some point. It took some time, but he eventually learned that even heroes have flaws, and by 1999, he had grown to forgive Blackie for what he had put his son through during his not-so-innocent preadolescent years.

Kiedis' forgiveness came in the form of 'Savior', a controlled and emotionally charged song that leans in the direction of continuous admiration instead of delayed absolution. 'Dusting off your saviour, forgiving any behaviour/He's just a man, all in a hand', sings Kiedis during the chorus that opens the song – offering the first hint of letting sleeping dogs lie. 'You were always my favourite', he continues earnestly before admitting to his father how, at long last, 'To celebrate you is greater now that I can'. That line on its own is powerful enough, and it is expressed with a courage that came from a lot of soul-searching in the build-up to what would become *Californication*.

'Savior' continues the album's second wind, and the song is ideally placed in the tracklisting in terms of the overall flow. Alongside the glistening electric guitar riffs, Flea's catchy bass notes and Chad Smith's snappy drum sections, John Frusciante performs a host of cameos, including some bluesy, almost country-like twangs during the song's dramatic intro. There are also a couple of interesting and leftfield psychedelic sections, where dizzying guitar and backing vocals meld with hypnotic shakers. At the same time, Kiedis reels off a peculiar rap ('We are the red hots and we're loving up the love me nots/The flowers in your flowerpots are dancing on the tabletops') that builds towards the latest memorable line aimed in the direction of his patriarch – 'And now I see you in a beautiful and different light/He's just a man and everything he does will be alright'. There is a lot to like about 'Savior', which again sounds unlike any other Red Hot Chili Peppers song, past or present.

Blackie Dammett eventually secured a career (of sorts) in acting, with his first role being a small one in a 1977 episode of *Charlie's Angels*. Minor parts in episodes of *Starsky And Hutch*, *Magnum P.I.* and *The Fall Guy* followed, as well as in movies, most of which were made for TV. The most ironic of Dammett's roles came in the first *Lethal Weapon* movie, where he played a drug dealer. Getting into character for that one must have been easy.

For much of the 1990s, Dammett ran the Chilis' *Rockinfreakapotamus* fan club under the self-proclaimed guise of 'Head Honcho and Chief Potentate'. With the rise of the internet by the decade's end, the fan club was replaced by the band's official website, which incidentally won the Best Artist Website award at the 1999 MTV VMAs. Blackie Dammett passed away on 12 May 2021, aged 81.

'Purple Stain'

'Purple Stain', according to Anthony Kiedis, 'refers to a double entendre of a girl's hair dye staining your pillow and your girl's menstrual flow staining your everything'. How lovely.

Possessing certain similarities to songs found on *Blood Sugar Sex Magik*, 'Purple Stain' is another funk-fuelled rocker that, unlike 'Get On Top' and 'I Like Dirt' before it, has a little more depth, at least musically. John Frusciante's jagged verse riff is creative, while Flea's offbeat bass work is some of his best across the entire record.

There is a consistent midtempo pace for much of the song, where

Kiedis reels off lyrical passages that are, at times, flippant and otherwise random processions. Its title is a play on Prince's epic love ballad 'Purple Rain', however, Kiedis decides to apply his affection in a way that comes across as fatuous and a little nauseating. There are more pop culture references thrown in, too – as Kiedis did on the title track – as, this time, the frontman gives shoutouts to the classic British comedy group Monty Python, to Bram Stoker's vampire Dracula and bizarrely to Darla Hood, a much-loved child actress from the 1930s' short films *Our Gang*. The psychedelic Hendrix-esque chorus, where Kiedis' vocals have a hallucinogenic effect, has him stating the obvious – 'Cause we all live in Hollywood' – which is further in keeping with the album's overriding premise.

The primary focus of 'Purple Stain' deserves to be on its fantastic instrumentation. The first half of the song is good, but the second is sensational and instantly propels itself onto the *Californication* highlight reel. While Frusciante goes into overdrive with a piercing, effect-laden guitar solo, Chad Smith is let loose to perform his own insane drum salvo. The style and energy that he brings to the kit and continues to bring after over 30 years has allowed him to be included in conversations surrounding the greatest rock drummers; his blistering assault on 'Purple Stain' supplies solid evidence in supporting such claims. Setting his trusted ghost notes aside in favour of raw and infectious power, Smith smashes and crashes like a man possessed, his often-recognised fast right foot working at breakneck speed during a breathless and dynamic execution. Even so deep into *Californication*, each member of the Red Hot Chili Peppers continues to thrive.

'Right On Time'

A modern take (as of 1999) on the Red Hot Chili Peppers of old, 'Right On Time' ventures back to the frenetic funk-punk of the band's self-titled debut and the ensuing *Freaky Styley* and *Uplift Mofo Party Plan* albums. During this less than two-minute rager, Kiedis' animated rapping gloats over a cacophony of wah-infused guitar, a heavy zig-zagging bass riff and more explosive drum blasts.

In between those sonic swathes come moments of calm in which Kiedis smoothly repeats the song's title over and over again. Since his original arrival, Frusciante's backing vocals have brought a whole new aspect to the Red Hot Chili Peppers, so much so they have become part of the band's extremely distinctive style. His feathered harmonies work extremely well during these delightfully dreamy sequences, perfectly placed and expertly delivered as always, before the track returns to its riotous assault.

'Right On Time' is the album's final rock cut. In some ways, it feels like the song was thrown onto the tracklisting purely for the sake of it, but still, it is fun, energetic and enjoyable for the short time it hangs around.

'Road Trippin"

The entirely acoustic 'Road Trippin" is one of a very small handful of Red Hot Chili Peppers songs to not contain any drumming. Chad Smith may have been credited on the track, but it was he who decided the song sounded better without his involvement. When you dig a little deeper into the song, you can certainly see where Smith was coming from.

'Road Trippin" is a song about togetherness and brotherhood. It's a summery and reflective number that documents a trip Kiedis, Frusciante and Flea took after Frusciante had returned to the band. The lyrics are markedly void of metaphors, as Kiedis tells the story of his adventure along the Pacific Coast Highway to go surfing near Big Sur, 'With my two favourite allies/Fully loaded, we got snacks and supplies'. The story doesn't intentionally leave Chad Smith out of the equation; it was simply because the drummer wasn't into surfing, so he chose not to join in on the festivities that day.

'So much has come before those battles lost and won/This life is shining more forever in the sun' continues Kiedis, as Frusciante and Flea's delicate picked tones help paint a vivid and rhythmic scene. Patrick Warren guests on the track to contribute exquisite orchestral nuances via his Chamberlin organ, adding an emotive atmosphere to this chronicle of brotherly love.

It may not be the sound of the band that many came to love or expect of them over the years, but 'Road Trippin" would become a big fan favourite because of its wholly unusual approach. It was even released as the fifth single in late 2000/early 2001, but only in Australia and the UK. Jonathan Dayton and Valerie Faris returned to direct the music video, but perhaps because there was no single release in the US, it wasn't made available Stateside until it was included on the Chilis' 2003 *Greatest Hits* video collection. In the video, Kiedis, Frusciante and Flea hole themselves up in a beach house and perform the song as the sun glistens on the ocean behind them. The vibe is chilled, much like the track itself, as day turns to night, and with a fire lit, the trio simply relax and let go of all past complications. Chad Smith makes a brief appearance in the promo clip when he arrives at the beach on a rowboat and is greeted by his ecstatic bandmates.

Surprisingly, 'Road Trippin" has only ever been performed live on four occasions – twice in 2000 and twice in 2004. All four performances were from benefit concerts for the non-profit organisation Bridge School, which helps children with severe speech and physical impairments, at the Shoreline Amphitheatre in Mountain View, California.

With an allure shaped by simple chord progressions and an extended display of Frusciante's dulcet vocal tones, which, again, work perfectly alongside Kiedis' lead, 'Road Trippin" provides a serene end to a quite remarkable Red Hot Chili Peppers album.

Official B-sides
'Fat Dance'

In 2006, a remastered version of *Californication* was made purchasable on iTunes; along with the standard album came three bonus tracks. The first of those was 'Fat Dance', a meaty funk rocker straight out of the *Blood Sugar Sex Magik* playbook. Anthony Kiedis delivers a commanding rap vocal, where, once again, he declares his love for then-girlfriend Yohanna Logan. At times naughty ('Kitchen or bedroom or bathroom floor/Keep it moving because I need the hardcore') and at times showing pure affection ('Oh Yohanna love, my Yohanna love/She was just the cutest thing, my God, that I have ever seen'), Kiedis' feelings are portrayed over an uncompromising barrage of jagged funk riffs and deep bass grooves. Musically, 'Fat Dance' is very much in the style of 'Give It Away' and 'Suck My Kiss' and based on *Californication* cuts like 'Get On Top' and 'I Like Dirt' – this one could easily have joined them on the album's final tracklisting.

'Over Funk'

Possibly more in the style of Parliament-Funkadelic, or even Prince, than the harder funk rock the Chilis had been producing over the years, 'Over Funk' is a snappy but fairly standard song in which Flea is the dominant player. He brings the throbbing pulse with an effective bass riff while, for once, John Frusciante's finger-picked notes sound more reserved. The song's lyrical content sounds like it was made up on the spot, but Kiedis still manages to bring a smile to faces with random rhymes bereft of depth or meaning. The line, 'Go ballistic, anarchistic, smack my mouth and then you kissed it', offers a strong case in point. 'Over Funk' never really moves out of second gear, and although it did appear on the iTunes remaster in its fully finished form, one cannot imagine the song ever being a serious contender for a spot on the official album release.

'Quixoticelixer'

Anthony Kiedis fought tooth and nail to have 'Californication' on the record, having faced strong resistance from the rest of the band from the outset. But in getting his way, it seems Kiedis was forced to relegate another track to free up room, and 'Quixoticelixer' is believed to have been the unfortunate victim to make way. Had the song featured on *Californication*, it could have been a hit, but instead, it can simply be considered an outstanding B-side.

With its title combining the words 'Quixotic' and 'Elixir' – the former explored in Miguel De Cervantes' epic early 17th-century novel, which surrounded idealism, *Don Quixotic*, and the latter referring to magical or medicinal potions – Kiedis covers similar themes in the song's prodigious lyrics. It's ironic that 'Californication' has been considered by many as the song to showcase Kiedis' best lyric writing because 'Quixoticelixer' could have given the title track a run for its money had it received similar infamy back in 1999. 'Kick back a little just to watch and see, getting sicker by the minute with debauchery' is the first of many interesting lines where Kiedis appears to be in love with something or someone. It's probably a bit of both, if truth be told, the something in this instance likely relating to the singer's battles with addiction. 'The madder the boy, the sadder the song/ That's a wicked fate but the sick get strong' attests to him overcoming his struggles before 'Everyday depression in a beautiful dress/Lady made a beautiful mess I guess' finds him shifting his attention towards his other compulsion – women.

'Quixoticelixer' flows at a leisurely pace and is littered with melodic flourishes. The intricately layered backing vocals add a whole new dynamic, especially in the latter half when Kiedis raps over John Frusciante's harmonic reinforcements. Another extended playout grows more intense thanks to its absorbing rhythm section, while the chorus exudes power through its sparsity – just a modest hook that you can't help but sing along to after the very first listen. To say it was made for the radio airwaves is an understatement.

'Quixoticelixer' isn't quite on the level of 'Californication', nor the album's other big hits 'Scar Tissue' and 'Otherside', but it isn't far off.

'Terrible is a soul, when she told me that there is such a thing/Do you know that you glow when you go from winter to spring' is another of Kiedis' more effective lyrical entries and one that was deserving of being in a song intended to feature on the album. Kiedis hinted as much, although briefly, in his *Scar Tissue* memoir when he described 'Quixoticelixer' as one he had high hopes for before it ultimately ended up in the 'trash bin'.

It may have taken seven years, but the song finally got its deserved release on the iTunes remaster, and it is conceivable that some would fall in love with *Californication* all over again because of this brilliant and welcome addition.

'Gong Li'

Appearing as a B-side on the 'Scar Tissue' single and as a bonus track on the Japanese release of *Californication*, 'Gong Li' is named after the popular Chinese actress who has won multiple international awards for her roles in such films as *Farewell My Concubine* and *Memoirs Of A Geisha*. As a side note, 'Gong Li' loosely translates to 'Fuck You' in Mandarin.

The Chilis utilise some interesting time signatures here, building moderate tension and conflict in the overly Eastern-influenced sequences that are made up of spiralling guitar and bass riffs. Juxtaposed with airy, melodic alt rock verses that the quartet would become renowned for in the 2000s and beyond, Anthony Kiedis uses 'Gong Li' to continue his heartfelt bromance with John Frusciante. 'Some people say you hate me/I don't believe it's true, things that you're going through', he sings, as he considers the pair's reconciliation after the guitarist had successfully kicked his drug habits. While there isn't a great deal of lyrical content, the message is clear and sobering. 'I'm not afraid to know, when things are getting low', Kiedis continues, speaking from experience it seems, as Frusciante's slick guitar work acts as his own form of response and support.

'Gong Li' is a popular track in the Red Hot Chili Peppers cannon, and through featuring on the 'Scar Tissue' single, it offered the first hint of the sheer depth in quality of the songs the quartet were coming out with during those *Californication* sessions.

'Instrumental #1' (Frusciante, Balzary, Smith)

The second B-side to arrive on the 'Scar Tissue' single is, from what John Frusciante referred to during a 2004 interview, an improvised jam between himself, Flea and Chad Smith. Frusciante also stated that the naturally titled 'Instrumental #1' was only played once and went in a direction he wished he could have explored further.

The track is not a funk exposé. Instead, it is moody, soulful and penetrative. Frusciante's guitar work is extremely experimental, but it is Flea's wiry bassline that you cannot help but be drawn to. It feels almost progressive and resoundingly hypnotic, and the stamina the bassist shows in repeating the riff for the entire three minutes of the track's runtime is absolutely incredible.

No vocals were required on this powerful composition, which, in truth, is another Red Hot Chili Peppers song that sounds wholly original. With that said, it's a shame we will never hear the instrumental as part of a fully realised song or, indeed, find out what Anthony Kiedis could have brought to the table from his side. On its own, though, 'Instrumental #1' is a stellar piece of music.

'Instrumental #2' (Frusciante, Balzary, Smith)
Rounding off the Australian edition of *Californication*, 'Instrumental #2' is another joyous display of musical dexterity. Frusciante stars with some slick chord changes and mini shreds, as well as his typically clean-cut funk and blues-tinged riffs. Flea's smooth bassline supplies a perfect undertone. Chad Smith's drumming is particularly animated in comparison to his more restrained efforts on '#1'. Once again, this is the sound of a trio of musicians who were having fun in the studio, jamming together and seeing what came to fruition.

'Teatro Jam' (Frusciante, Balzary, Smith)
As the title suggests, 'Teatro Jam' was born during the Chilis' demo sessions with Daniel Lanois at Teatro Studios in September 1998. This is understandably raw and rough around the edges, and it is a lot heavier, too. Frusciante uses fuzz and distortion pedals to create some sonic guitar artistry, which is actually in a similar vein to Led Zeppelin, just to give an idea of its sound and style. Flea and Smith are happy to provide ample backup on this one, allowing Frusciante to lead the way with his usual verve – his grinding riffs and explosive rhythms offering a lesson in elite improvisation.

'Teatro Jam' was later used as a B-side on the 'Around The World' single, where it was deservedly given its moment to shine.

'Slowly Deeply' (Frusciante, Balzary, Smith)
This latest instrumental unmasks a lethal dose of metallic funk and is another of the Chilis' heaviest arrangements. Flea's fat bass groove

instantly brings Tim Commerford of Rage Against the Machine and Les Claypool of Primus to mind, while Frusciante's crunching riffs sit somewhere in the region of grunge stalwarts Alice in Chains. Certain parts of this track even sound like the bridge of Alice's 'Angry Chair', which can be found on their seminal 1992 album *Dirt*. Later, a discordant guitar solo provides the icing on the cake as the track draws to its colossal climax.

'Slowly Deeply' was belatedly released as a B-side on the 'Universally Speaking' single in 2003, which was the fourth to be taken from the *By The Way* album. The *Californication* follow-up landed in the summer of 2002 and found the Red Hot Chili Peppers moving further away from their funk roots in favour of subdued and overly melodic alt rock songs. 'Universally Speaking' seamlessly underlined the band's intentions, but including the disparate 'Slowly Deeply' as its B-side still feels like a strange choice, not just because of how it sounded but because it was written and recorded during a different era entirely.

'How Strong'

A B-side on the other side of the 'Otherside' single, and also part of the extended Australian edition of *Californication*, 'How Strong' is another excellent song that, for one reason or another, failed to warrant a spot on the official album release.

Its vibe is actually more *One Hot Minute* than it is *Californication*, being slightly moodier and moving along at a methodical pace. Flea's pure funk bass is built around warping riffs, with a bit of wah pedal used for greater effect, and John Frusciante is back in his own little world, experimenting with his guitar and emitting plenty of captivating rhythms. Anthony Kiedis continually asks the question, 'How strong is my love?', before it appears that the woman of his desires becomes one of the few to shun his advances – 'Lord, I can't believe she turned me down/She turned me inside out'.

Following an often tried and tested formula, where the Chilis slowly build towards a grand finale, it's when a psychedelic bridge changes the song's course that you have the feeling that something special is coming. Presenting power through simplicity, Frusciante unveils a sublime single-note solo that only he could come up with. The ear-splitting feedback enhances the tension already generated as the bass continues to gyrate and a staccato drum section reaffirms the song's fundamentals.

This final flurry, where Kiedis repeatedly sings the chorus line, is engrossing to the last; it is songs such as 'How Strong' that led to a number of Red Hot Chili Peppers fans remarking on various message boards that they felt some of the B-sides were actually better than the majority of the official album tracks. 'How Strong' is an absolute gem and the same can be said of 'Bunker Hill'...

'Bunker Hill'

Given the full title of 'These Are Not My Dreams Of Bunker Hill' at its demo stage and then shortened to just 'Bunker Hill' later on, this song is believed to have been the first written by the quartet after John Frusciante re-joined the lineup.

Its sound is evidently unlike the rest of the *Californication* tracks, where lighter and lush guitar melodies are far more comparable to those found on the *By The Way* album. Flea's gloriously groovy and insanely catchy bassline really sets the scene from the off before 'Bunker Hill' reveals more of its appeal at every turn. Anthony Kiedis' lyrics are, like on so many other occasions, self-contained. However, the theme of love appears to be the order of the day – none more so than during the stadium-sized chorus ('Are you coming through, do you want me to, take your body/It would be so cool, to be cool with you'). It's crazy to think this song was shelved, considering that it possesses all the qualities of a potentially successful single: Frusciante's beautiful backing vocals, a guitar solo, a classic Chilis instrumental outro and an infectious, alluring hook.

While plotting their *Greatest Hits* album in 2003, the Chilis wrote and recorded two new songs, which were incorporated into the tracklisting. One of those songs was the instantly likeable 'Fortune Faded', and when it was released as a single, 'Bunker Hill' was chosen as one of the B-sides. For a while, a proportion of fans thought the track was written during the *By The Way* sessions, and they could have been forgiven for thinking as much. Nevertheless, they were wrong, and to this day, on fan forums and online message boards, 'Bunker Hill' still gets a hell of a lot of love. With a degree of frustration and disbelief, the question of 'How was this song only ever a B-side?' remains a hot topic of debate, and it isn't just 'Bunker Hill' that people speak so highly of. Whether it's 'Quixoticelixer', 'How Strong' or even some of the instrumentals, it is apparent that the Red Hot Chili Peppers have written a lot of B-sides that are actually better than many of their A-sides. 'Bunker Hill', however, may just be the best of them all.

Single Releases And Tracklistings

'Scar Tissue'
CD Single:
1. 'Scar Tissue'
2. 'Gong Li'
3. 'Instrumental #1'

Slipcase CD Single:
1. 'Scar Tissue'
2. 'Gong Li'

Cassette Single:
1. 'Scar Tissue'
2. 'Gong Li'

'Around The World'
CD 1:
1. 'Around The World'
2. 'Parallel Universe' (demo)
3. 'Teatro Jam'

CD 2:
1. 'Around The World'
2. 'Me And My Friends' (live recording)
3. 'Yertle Trilogy' (live recording)

Maxi-single:
1. 'Around The World'
2. 'Parallel Universe' (demo)
3. 'Teatro Jam'

'Otherside'
CD 1:
1. 'Otherside'
2. 'How Strong'

CD 2:
1. 'Otherside'
2. 'My Lovely Man' (live recording)
3. 'Around The World' (music video)

Californication Red Hot Chili Peppers

CD 3 (Australian Release):
1. 'Otherside'
2. 'How Strong'
3. 'My Lovely Man' (live recording)
4. 'Road Trippin" (minus strings)
5. 'Scar Tissue' (music video)
6. 'Around The World' (music video)

CD 4:
1. 'Otherside'
2. 'How Strong'
3. 'My Lovely Man' (live recording)
4. 'Road Trippin" (minus strings)

CD 5:
1. 'Otherside'
2. 'How Strong'
3. 'Road Trippin" (minus strings)
4. 'Otherside' (music video)

Cassette (US Release):
1. 'Otherside'
2. 'How Strong'

'Californication'
CD 1:
1. 'Californication'
2. 'I Could Have Lied' (live recording)
3. 'End Of Show Brisbane' (live recording)

CD 2:
1. 'Californication'
2. 'I Could Have Lied' (live recording)
3. 'End Of Show State College' (live recording)

EP:
1. 'Californication'
2. 'End Of Show Brisbane' (live recording)
3. 'I Could Have Lied' (live recording)
4. 'End Of Show State College' (live recording)

'Road Trippin"
CD 1:
1. 'Road Trippin"
2. 'Californication' (live recording)
3. 'Blood Sugar Sex Magik' (live recording)
4. 'Road Trippin" (enhanced video)

CD 2:
1. 'Road Trippin"
2. 'Under The Bridge' (live recording)
3. 'If You Have To Ask' (live recording)

CD 3:
1. 'Road Trippin"
2. 'Californication' (live recording)
3. 'Blood Sugar Sex Magik' (live recording)
4. 'Under The Bridge' (live recording)

Australian Single:
1. 'Road Trippin"
2. 'Californication' (live recording)
3. 'Blood Sugar Sex Magik' (live recording)
4. 'Under The Bridge' (live recording)
5. 'If You Have To Ask' (live recording)

Californication Red Hot Chili Peppers

The Teatro Sessions

Located in Oxnard and around an hour's drive from Central LA, Teatro Studio was originally known as the Boulevard Theater when it first opened its doors in 1929. In the 1960s, the place was turned into a Spanish language theatre, where it thrived for three decades before finally closing its doors in 1993. Two years later, Daniel Lanois and his buddy Mark Howard decided to rent the building for $1500 a month and turn it into a recording studio. Only two albums were ever credited as being recorded at Teatro, the first being Bob Dylan's 1997 effort *Time Out Of Mind*. Although the final versions of the songs were actually put to tape at Criteria Studios in Miami, the demos recorded at Teatro were integral in inspiring the album's overall sound.

Time Out Of Mind became Dylan's first platinum-certified record since *Slow Train Coming* – released in 1979 – and at the 1998 Grammy's, the album won three awards, including the coveted Album of the Year gong.

In September 1998, Willie Nelson's 45th studio album gave the studio further notoriety when the artist chose to name his latest work after the very place of its creation. *Teatro* even used the front of the building for its cover art, where Nelson's name can be seen emblazoned on the large marquee. Iggy Pop, Marianne Faithful and Emmylou Harris also frequented Teatro for various rehearsal and demo sessions before the Red Hot Chili Peppers went in and recorded two discs' worth of their own material. The quartet were firmly in the zone at the time of their visit, and on one particularly fruitful day, they were able to record 11 tracks. Overall, the Chilis used up four reels of tape containing a host of pieces at various stages of progress. Some were simply vocal tracks, some were instrumentals, while others featured full songs that appeared very close to completion. Here is a brief rundown of the seven previously unheard songs that were part of the online leak that occurred in 2014.

'Andaman & Nicobar'

A short two-minute dose of vibrant punk 'n' roll, 'Andaman & Nicobar' is built around a groovy riff and a rolling drum loop. The track contains two small vocal passages, however, Anthony Kiedis' lyrics aren't easily audible. Researching them online is just as hard a task, as those who have previously attempted it have left plenty of blanks and question marks. The fact the song's title seems to have been taken from islands in an Indian union territory fails to shed any further light on a potential theme, either. Musically, this isn't a bad track, but the Chilis quickly binned it and so this demo remains the only evidence of its existence.

'Boatman'
Another decent instrumental where John Frusciante reels off a host of spritely riffs, 'Boatman' reveals itself to be a conventional Red Hot Chili Peppers jam. Its flow remains consistent for much of the four-minute running time, with Flea and Chad Smith playing along to Frusciante's lead with a modest bass riff and a subtle beat. Out of nowhere comes a frenzied burst of distorted delight, where a rasping guitar solo fights a pounding drum section for ultimate dominance. This welcome flourish doesn't last for long before the original flow returns to see things out, but that 20-second surge of sonic fury is worth the price of admission alone.

'Mommasan'
One of the few demos with the potential to have been something more, 'Mommasan' is a brilliant Red Hot Chili Peppers song that possesses elements of the overall *Californication* vibe. Solid guitar-driven rock, a little Hendrix-like with its psychedelic guitar textures and a bass funk shimmering underneath – the music sets the scene for Kiedis' combination of rapping and singing. The song's chorus is a big highlight, of which Kiedis appears to dedicate to his mother ('Oh momma please don't cry/I promise I won't die and if I stay too long, well I will be forever in your favour') over a melodic rhythm section. 'Mommasan' sways one way and then another but the control is always there, and during another captivating instrumental part, Frusciante comes up with another stunning and emotional guitar solo. In binning 'Mommasan', it really feels like the Red Hot Chili Peppers missed a trick here.

'Plate Of Brown'
'Plate Of Brown' is a reflective interlude-like instrumental where Frusciante experiments with a selection of finger-picked notes and riffs. There isn't much else going on, in all honesty, and Flea and Smith once again play only minimalistic roles. Lounge music may be the best way to describe this rather chilled segue.

'Tellin' A Lie'
Like 'Mommasan', 'Tellin' A Lie' is full of promise and should really have been explored further. This beautiful ballad, with verse guitar

melodies that are particularly pretty and thoughtful, perfectly supports Kiedis' emotionally fraught lyrics: 'Would you believe I'm tellin' a lie, would you believe that it's just a disguise/I don't invent myself to shelter 'cause the fame won't kill me', he sings resolutely. For a demo performance, his vocal is so effective that it could have been used on the master mix had 'Tellin' A Lie' become the song it perhaps deserved to be. It's worthy of repeated listens.

'Trouble In The Pub'
This unfinished rap funk track would go on to be dissected and parts of it used on the 'Fat Dance' B-side. Kiedis' humorous rhyming shines on the primitive line, 'I met her in the schoolyard, and she was such a cool card/She took me for a fool, 'cause I'm acting like a retard', which is about as substantial as the lyrics get. Instrumental passages make up most of the track, with short solos and funk riffs playing off against each other.

'Sugar Sugar'
'Sugar Sugar' is a quick-fire funk number driven by John Frusciante's rapid, jangly riffing. This song is a lot of fun to listen to, but you do get the feeling that the band had already decided it wasn't going to get past the demo stage. Even so, the dedication in Frusciante's and Flea's playing is unquestionable. As with most of the Teatro tracks, it is Frusciante's guitar work that makes them such imperative listening, and his proficient performance on 'Sugar Sugar' supplies another standout moment.

'Funky Jam'
Exactly what its title suggests, this eight-minute instrumental jam could almost be a John Frusciante solo track. His guitar-playing repertoire is on full show throughout, from his trademark finger-picked riffs to heavier jousts funded by distortion, fuzz and reverb. 'Funky Jam' is an ideal demonstration of the art of playing funk rock, and it must have been an absolute blast to have witnessed Frusciante, Flea and Smith ad-libbing in the studio. This is just one example of the trio creating magic together.

The Californication Tour

As the release of *Californication* drew closer, the Red Hot Chili Peppers announced a handful of free shows across America at selected high school proms. With the continual advancement of technology and especially the internet, where more and more young people were logging on to computers and surfing their lives away, the Chilis replaced their *Rockinfreakapotamus* fan club with a brand spanking new website, which, in turn, offered easier access into the world of the rejuvenated four-piece. Furthermore, playing such events as proms was an ideal way for the band to re-integrate themselves with a key target audience, but before the Chilis could hit the road, America was sent into mourning.

On 20 April 1999, Eric Harris and Dylan Klebold acted out their year-long plan of destruction at their Columbine High School. On a day like any other before it, the 12th-grade outcasts arrived on site just after 11 am, armed with a plethora of guns, knives and handmade explosives. For reasons unknown at the time, their sole intention was to commit mass murder. When their bombs failed to detonate, Harris and Klebold resorted to their secondary weaponry and mercilessly fired at their fellow students. Along with those who suffered gunshot wounds and other injuries sustained while attempting to flee the chaos, 12 students and a teacher lost their lives on that fateful day. Less than one hour after the rampage began, the two perpetrators killed themselves with self-inflicted gunshots to the head.

At the time, the so-called 'Columbine Massacre' had the infamy of being the deadliest school shooting in American history. The events of that day would go on to inspire future school shootings, and in a country that has had extremely questionable gun control laws for way too long, such attacks on innocent children – often committed by children themselves – have sadly become far more common over the years.

With America still reeling, the Red Hot Chili Peppers embarked on their planned tour between 15-27 May. However, the concept of the shows had now changed and the message being issued was to 'stop the hate'. Referred to as the *Teen Tolerance Tour*, the Chilis visited Portland, Seattle, Minneapolis, Pontiac and Philadelphia and played to students whose price of admission was to present suggestions on how to put an end to hatred, bullying and violence in high schools. For a couple of weeks at least, the whole of America stood with the Red Hot Chili Peppers in support of the message the band were trying to achieve. The 15 May show would see the live debuts of a

Californication Red Hot Chili Peppers

number of *Californication* songs, while some others had already been unveiled on the quartet's previous tour at the back end of 1998.

At the beginning of June, the Chilis flew to Europe for a small promotional jaunt. After one-off stops in Germany, Sweden, France and Italy, they moved over to the UK where, first, they visited the renowned Maida Vale Studios in London. The band recorded a four-song live session consisting of 'Emit Remmus', 'Scar Tissue', 'Parallel Universe' and the *Blood Sugar Sex Magik* B-side 'Soul To Squeeze', which later aired on Simon Mayo's Radio 1 show. TV performances on the BBC's *Top Of The Pops* and Channel 4's *TFI Friday* continued to support the already popular 'Scar Tissue' single before the Chilis signed off with a full show at the 1500-capacity Camden Palace.

With the hype surrounding *Californication*, the Red Hot Chili Peppers re-established themselves as major players in the rock world, and some of their biggest shows as of 1999 were fast approaching. A couple of sets on radio station-sponsored festivals found the quartet rightfully returning to headline status, as they did for a Musicians Assistance Program and Hereditary Disease Foundation benefit concert at the Hollywood Palladium on 25 June. The band's next destination was then Woodstock.

As had the previous event in 1994, Woodstock '99 attempted to emulate the iconic 1969 festival. With a lineup featuring The Who, Janis Joplin, Jefferson Airplane and Jimi Hendrix, to name just a few, the original Woodstock didn't just emphasise the decade's hippie counterculture; it also provided a pivotal moment in music history. Not only was a community formed through a shared love of music, but the fallout surrounding the Vietnam War, which was going on at the same time, allowed people from all backgrounds to come together and promote peace and unity. However, 30 years later, people's mindsets had dramatically changed, and the 'Peace and Music' slogan Woodstock had always prided itself on had far less relevancy as the new millennium approached.

The extended four-day event in 1999 took place between 22-25 July at the former Griffiss Air Force Base in Rome, New York. The choice of location – an old airport hangar offering very little shade, booked in the peak of summer and with a crowd of 400,000 people attending across the four days – was a precursor that something might go terribly wrong before the weekend was over. But the lineup was stellar, and diverse, and anyone due to attend the festival would no doubt have been excited about the quality of acts who were set to perform. For fans of hip hop, there was DMX, Ice Cube, Everlast and the Roots. Lovers of old-school funk were salivating over James Brown and George Clinton & the P-Funk All-Stars. Hardcore metalheads were ready to throw their horns up for two of the genre's biggest thrash acts – Metallica and Megadeth, and with the rise of nu metal, Korn, Limp Bizkit, Kid Rock, Godsmack and Sevendust all had a platform to reach bigger audiences than ever before. The Red Hot Chili Peppers were booked to headline the East Stage on Sunday evening – their set expected to draw Woodstock '99 to a triumphant close and enter another legendary festival into the record books. It became legendary, but it would be for all the wrong reasons.

Trouble had begun long before the Chilis even arrived in New York state; in fact, a proportion of attendees were left feeling disgruntled as soon as they walked through the entrance gates for the first time. Food and drink were forbidden from being brought on site, and as people melted in 100°F temperatures, their blood only boiled further when seeing the criminally overpriced festival vendors. Four dollars for a bottle of water was a ludicrous sum for such a necessity, and by the final day, when stocks were running low, prices across many of the stalls had quadrupled. It quickly became apparent that there was a sheer lack of security across the 3,600-acre site, with some taking the job purely to get into the festival for free. As soon as they were in, off came their uniforms and into the crowds they went. There were also nowhere near enough toilets for the volume of attendees, and sanitation was disgustingly poor.

Members of the crowds had already been playing up for a number of artists by throwing bottles and other missiles towards the stages on regular occasions, but the first real spark of disorder came during Limp Bizkit's raucous set on Saturday afternoon. The rap-metal five-piece had recently reached superstar status with their second album, *Significant Other*, topping the *Billboard* 200. When the band launched into the hard-hitting and defiant 'Break Stuff', the crowd literally followed suit. Twelve-foot plywood boards had been erected around the site perimeter to try and foil gate-crashing issues that had marred the previous events, and now they were being torn down by a select number of savage festivalgoers. Limp Bizkit's enigmatic frontman, Fred Durst, was instantly blamed for inciting the mini-riot that ensued, and he wouldn't be the last artist to be made a scapegoat in the coming days. Over the course of the long weekend, three people died – two of them due to heat exhaustion/hyperthermia – and a number of sexual assaults were reported to have occurred in both the crowds and the campsites.

Californication Red Hot Chili Peppers

By Sunday evening, many of those who remained were tired, dirty, overheated and severely aggravated. Much of the Red Hot Chili Peppers' set went without incident, as the quartet (featuring a completely naked Flea) rifled through *Californication* cuts, including 'Around The World', 'Easily' and the glorious album title track. Earlier in the day, the anti-gun violence organisation PAX had been issuing candles from an onsite booth, having planned a vigil for the victims of the Columbine massacre. Without seeking authorisation from festival organisers or notifying the local fire brigade, the candles were directed to be lit as soon as the Chilis launched into 'Under The Bridge', which the band always played towards the end of their set. Most of those taking part in the vigil acted in a sensible manner, but others used the candles to literally set Woodstock on fire. In Anthony Kiedis' memoir, he noted how, as soon as the band arrived at the festival, he could see that something was very wrong:

> When we pulled up onto this old military base way up in upstate New York, it was clear that this situation had nothing to do with Woodstock anymore. It wasn't symbolic of peace and love but of greed and cashing in. The little dove with the flower in its mouth was saying, 'How much can we overcharge the kids for this T-shirt and get away with it?'

For the band's encore, they were asked by Jimi Hendrix's half-sister, Janie, if they could perform a cover of 'Fire' as a tribute to Hendrix's classic headline performance at Woodstock '69. The Chilis were already accustomed to the song, having recorded a studio version to be included on their 1989 album *Mother's Milk*. At one point, and with the crowd getting more out of control, Kiedis was asked by event coordinators to try and calm down the crowd, but his requests fell on deaf ears. As their set was about to come to a close, and with the most genuine of intentions, the Red Hot Chili Peppers launched into the last song of the evening and the last song of Woodstock '99 – 'Fire'. By now, Plywood had been thrown onto heaps of litter and set alight, an audio tower caught fire and eventually collapsed and rabid troublemakers broke into merch booths and ATMs and looted them. The Chilis were blamed for fuelling tensions by playing 'Fire', while in the aftermath of the festival, shocking scenes of warzone-like destruction were cast across news stories both on TV and in print across the globe. The most famous line written by any journalist came from the pen of the *San Francisco Examiner*'s Jane Ganahl, who described Woodstock Sunday as 'The day the music died'. In Kiedis' memoir, he continued to reminisce about the festival, remembered how his band were accused of inciting the late-night carnage and wondered if they could have done things differently that day:

> We ignored those ridiculous charges, though it did turn out that the promoters were assholes and it had not been a user-friendly environment. We should have paid closer attention to that and not been so isolated from the fan's point of view. I guess it was irresponsible to just show up, play and leave without taking a closer look at some of the details surrounding the show.

In 2021, a documentary titled *Woodstock '99: Peace, Love And Rage* aired on the HBO network, and it was clear that much of the blame deserved to be placed at the feet of the festival's organisers, Michael Lang and John Scher. If anything, they riled up the crowds as much as any artist did through repeatedly cutting costs and using sub-contractors for onsite amenities, who were able to charge however much as they wanted for food and drink. The Offspring also played Woodstock '99, and in the documentary, the punk band's guitarist, Kevin 'Noodles' Wasserman, shared his own explicit thoughts on the festival:

> You know, there was a festival in Germany that was literally built by Hitler, and we've played there a bunch of times: great venue and a bunch of fun. That airbase was less hospitable than a place built by Nazis.

After Woodstock, the Red Hot Chili Peppers recharged their batteries before they returned to Europe in mid-August for the remainder of the summer festival season. The band's most high-profile shows came at the Leeds and Reading extravaganzas, where they headlined the third and final days. In early October, they moved over to South America and performed shows on consecutive nights in Chile and Argentina, as well as single dates in Brazil and, finally, Mexico. On 26 October, they popped to New York City to play in front of 300 WXRK-FM radio competition winners on the observation deck on top of the World Trade Center. The Red Hot Chili Peppers had indeed reached new heights. For the next month, the band were back in Europe to feed the insatiable appetites of more of their overseas fans. They

Californication Red Hot Chili Peppers

played in Finland, Norway, Sweden and Germany, as well as the Netherlands, Switzerland, Italy, France and Spain, before a one-off date in London on 6 November saw the quartet fill the 12,500-capacity Wembley Arena.

The annual *Billboard* Music Awards took place at the MGM Grand Garden Arena in Las Vegas on 8 December. Esteemed rock acts including Creed, Metallica and The Offspring all took home various prizes that night, while the Red Hot Chili Peppers received an exclusive award to commemorate 'Scar Tissue' spending a then-record 16 weeks at the top of the Modern Rock Tracks chart. The quartet also performed the song during the ceremony before they were joined onstage by hip-hop superstar Snoop Dogg to play a cover of the 1974 Funkadelic track 'Red Hot Mama'.

After a celebratory New Year's Eve concert at the Great Western Forum in Inglewood, California, the Chilis prepared to next fly over to Japan in what would be the first time they had visited the Far East with John Frusciante in tow since the guitarist's acrimonious departure back in 1992. For three nights, the band shook the rafters of the famous Budokan, a martial arts hall-turned-concert venue that, since 1966, had hosted the likes of The Beatles, ABBA, Bob Dylan, Cheap Trick and KISS. In early January, the Red Hot Chili Peppers added their name to an illustrious honour roll, and as part of the setlists, which changed around a little with each show, 'Around The World', 'Scar Tissue', 'Otherside', 'I Like Dirt', 'Californication' and 'Right On Time' were played on all three nights. 'Easily' was played on two of those occasions and 'Parallel Universe' made an appearance during the final show.

For much of the 1990s, Anthony Kiedis was lodged in a rivalry of sorts with Mike Patton from Faith No More. The bands, who both featured strong funk elements in their music, had previously hit the road together on a leg of *The Uplift Mofo Party Plan* tour in 1987, as they continued to try and get their names out to the masses. Back then, though, both lineups were significantly different. By 1988, the Chilis were beginning to earn some long-awaited attention, and Faith No More, who themselves had been active for a decade at this point, were about to make their own breakthrough. The San Francisco-based five-piece had just fired their frontman, Chuck Mosley, and replaced him with the relatively unknown Patton. But in Patton, Faith No More had unmasked an extremely dexterous vocalist. Coming from a heavy metal background, Patton's screaming and guttural growls were already on point, but the man could also rap. His nasally singing, while possessing a childish impurity, also reflected a confidence that quickly endeared him to many.

Faith No More rocketed to prominence on the back of their 1989 album *The Real Thing*, which featured an incredibly eclectic set of songs. From the orchestral churn of 'Woodpecker From Mars' to the battle-hardened heavy metal onslaught of 'Surprise! You're Dead!', not to ignore the uncomfortable evocation of lounge music during 'Edge Of The World', Faith No More had turned the tables on what a hard rock or heavy metal record should sound like. But it was the album's surprise package of 'Epic' – made up of unconventional rap metal – which steered the band towards mainstream notoriety. It was the song's music video which ultimately triggered the hostility between Kiedis and Patton, which every now and then reared its head throughout the 1990s and into the early months of the new millennium.

In the video, Patton's dance moves and facial expressions struck a nerve with Kiedis, who would publicly state how he felt Patton was imitating his style. Patton's rap/scat vocal also appeared to irk the Chilis frontman, and while some may have viewed Patton's actions as a sign of respect or influence, Kiedis didn't. It was hardly loggerheads at dawn, but the two unquestionably talented singers would remonstrate against one another in various interviews while the rest of the members of both bands chose to very much distance themselves from the fallout.

The feud – if you could call it that – appeared to die out as the decade progressed ... until 1999. By now, Patton had resurrected his pre-Faith band Mr. Bungle, and like the Red Hot Chili Peppers, the avant-garde metal troupe were signed to Warner Bros. Records. *Californication* was in the bag and ready to go, and Mr. Bungle had also completed work on their latest album, which coincidentally was titled *California*. Both were set to be released on the very same day. Warner chose to shelve *California* for a month because, from a business point of view, it made very little sense to release two albums with similar titles at the same time. The bands may have sounded entirely different from one another, but it just wasn't worth risking a PR nightmare. Whether or not the Chilis had first dibs because their status was higher is unknown, but *Californication* was indeed released on the originally declared 8 June, and the album sold like hotcakes. It may still have been successful had it been the one to get pushed back, but in the end, it was Mr. Bungle who were the ones made to suffer.

Californication Red Hot Chili Peppers

Just weeks later, the Red Hot Chili Peppers and Mr. Bungle were scheduled to appear on many of the same bills of a handful of festivals across Europe – until Anthony Kiedis stepped in. Being the headline act meant the Chilis had a bit of pull on who they were sharing a stage with, and when Kiedis threatened to back out of those festival appearances unless Mr. Bungle were removed, the organisers promptly adhered to his demands. Later in the year, and as part of their nationwide tour promoting *California*, Mr. Bungle rocked up to Clutch Cargo's in Pontiac, Michigan, on Halloween. The perfect time of the year for many to dress up in scary and ghoulish costumes, Mr. Bungle decided to dress up as the Red Hot Chili Peppers for this show. Mike Patton was dressed as Anthony Kiedis – in Kiedis' home state – and repeatedly mocked the singer in various ways. Part of the band's set was even made up of cover medleys of 'Around The World', 'Give It Away', 'Scar Tissue' and 'Under The Bridge' before Mr. Bungle decided to take things even further. Mr. Bungle would allude to the Chilis' history of heroin abuse by pretending to shoot up onstage. Someone came out and acted as the ghost of Hillel Slovak, who had lost his life to the drug in 1988. The band even referenced River Phoenix – the popular Hollywood actor and friend of the Red Hot Chili Peppers – who died from a drug overdose outside the Viper Room in LA on 31 October 1993 while Flea and John Frusciante were performing with the alternative rock band P. In an interview undertaken during a documentary on Mr. Bungle's *California* album, guitarist Trey Spruance spoke of his frustration with the situation:

> It was pretty weird, having been fans of the first two Red Hot Chili Peppers albums, realising that somehow something personal had gone amiss somewhere. So amiss that a decade and a half after we'd liked this hugely popular band's music (and hadn't thought much about since), we'd be dealing with the fact that they were unmistakably trying to bury us. Why keep quiet?

Regardless of this, Bungle's distasteful actions that night, although brought on by frustration and confusion as to why they had been blackballed the previous summer, would ultimately lead to the band being removed from the Big Day Out lineup, which ran through New Zealand and Australia between 21 January-7 February 2000. Again, the demand had come from Anthony Kiedis; when asked why in a later interview, he simply responded, 'I would not have given two fucks if they played there with us. But after I heard about (the) Halloween show where they mocked us, fuck him (Patton) and fuck the whole band. I hope they all die.'

The ramifications proved to be terminal for Patton's mob, who missed out on performing alongside huge names such as Nine Inch Nails, Foo Fighters, Blink-182 and, of course, the Red Hot Chili Peppers in the cities of Auckland, Gold Coast, Brisbane, Sydney, Melbourne, Adelaide and Perth. Later in the year, Mr. Bungle would split up after the final show of their UK tour. The band's bassist, Trevor Dunn, placed the blame straight at the door of the Red Hot Chili Peppers for costing him and his bandmates a lot of money due to those missed festival appearances in Europe and Australia. Dunn also shared his disdain for Warner Bros. Records siding with the Chilis and especially for postponing the *California* album release. Looking back in a blog entry, Dunn spoke of his memories of the Pontiac show:

> I remember it was very funny to ridicule them without thinking about whether they would be aware or not. We were pretty pissed off for all the financial and personal damage that they caused to us based on their egos and freaks of power. We probably should have sued them.

After the Big Day Out run, the remainder of the *Californication* tour took place on home soil. From 24 May to 22 September, the Red Hot Chili Peppers performed in 39 states across the US, as well as taking on three further dates over the border in Canada. On 31 August, the quartet took a quick break from their headline tour to play a short set at the notorious Whisky a Go Go. As part of a special event put on by Los Angeles radio station KROQ, the band played six songs, including a cover of The Ramones' punk anthem 'Pinhead', while the other five were all taken from *Californication*. With a capacity of just 500, it is very rare that bigger bands return to the Whisky later in their careers, no matter what the venue had done for them in their early days, so having the Red Hot Chili Peppers play there in 2000 was a pretty big deal for both the venue and the lucky few hundred who were there to witness the show.

There were six legs of the *Californication* tour in total, which officially ran from 18 June 1999 to 22 September 2000. In that time, the quartet performed in 24 countries before the 135th and final show took place at the Key Arena in Seattle. The tour remains the band's biggest, and as well as grossing millions of dollars in revenue, it helped the Chilis break through to an even wider audience. In the 2000s, and with more successful albums behind them, including *By The Way* and the double-disc *Stadium Arcadium*, the Red Hot Chili Peppers' fan base continued to grow exponentially. The *Californication* tour had found the band playing in jampacked arenas, but their ever-increasing popularity has allowed them to move into stadium environments, where today, they regularly entertain the largest crowds of their entire career.

Woodstock '99 Setlist
'Around The World'
'Give It Away'
'Scar Tissue'
'Emit Remmus'
'Soul To Squeeze'
'If You Have To Ask'
'Suck My Kiss'
'Tiny Dancer' (Elton John Cover)
'Right On Time'
'Californication'
'My Lovely Man'
'Easily'
'Under The Bridge'
'Me And My Friends'
'Sir Psycho Sexy'
'Fire' (Jimi Hendrix Cover)

Reading Festival Setlist
'Around The World'
'Give It Away'
'Your Pussy's Glued To A Building On Fire (John Frusciante Solo Track)
'Scar Tissue'
'Suck My Kiss'
'Savior'
'I Like Dirt'
'If You Have To Ask'
'Soul To Squeeze'
'Organic Anti-Beat Box Band'
'Easily'

Californication Red Hot Chili Peppers

'Right On Time'
'Under The Bridge'
'Me And My Friends'
'Sir Psycho Sexy'
'The Power Of Equality'
'My Lovely Man'
'Search And Destroy' (Iggy Pop And The Stooges Cover)

Reception And Commercial Performance

In comparison to the underwhelming reaction that surrounded *One Hot Minute*, the reviews of *Californication* were far more positive. John Frusciante's return was cited by many critics as a key reason for the album's success, with his harmonies, melodies and overall masterful guitar work helping forge such strong instrumental passages. Anthony Kiedis also received high praise for the improved quality of the range, pitch and melodic sensibilities of his vocals and for his honest and inventive lyric writing.

Californication revitalised the Red Hot Chili Peppers. They had a settled lineup again, all members were generally sober and the creative peak they had experienced during the writing process in 1998 would spawn a host of great songs – some of which would become huge hits. The Chilis were also relevant again, having been tipped for greatness on the back of *Blood Sugar Sex Magik* at the turn of the decade. But after that, they slowly imploded, and although there were some good songs on *One Hot Minute*, the album hinted at a band who were teetering on the edge. *Californication* was just their second studio album to be released in eight years, but because the musical climate had drastically changed by 1999 – with nu metal and alternative rock now becoming accepted in the mainstream and leading rock's charge – the Red Hot Chili Peppers had a chance at salvation.

A week before the release of *Californication*, Shawn Fanning and Sean Parker boldly launched Napster. Taking advantage of the continually advancing capabilities of the internet, the duo developed the first user-friendly interface that allowed people to share MP3 music files with other users no matter where they were in the world. Napster became an overnight sensation, and at one point, the number of registered users of the service peaked at a staggering 80,000,000. As great as Napster was, or the idea behind it at least, it was also highly illegal. Users were able to come into possession of as much music as they wanted without having to pay a single penny, meaning artists and record labels lost out on a lot of money. The ramifications were enormous, with some labels folding and artists getting dropped because of poor commercial performances after their music had leaked ahead of the official release. Some even had completed albums permanently shelved, and because their label owned the rights to the material, this prevented the artist from ever being able to release the music – even after their working relationship was over. It didn't take long for Napster to encounter legal difficulties, primarily over copyright infringement, with lawsuits being filed against them by some of the biggest names in the business. Metallica, Dr. Dre and A&M Records were just a few of those who fought and won their cases to get Napster shut down. But, by the time the service folded in September 2002, the damage to the music industry and other entertainment sectors, which were also falling victim to internet piracy, was irreversible.

Californication arrived a week after Napster's inauguration, and while the Red Hot Chili Peppers may not have suffered as much as other artists back then, the songs from the album will no doubt have been uploaded and shared many a time. Nevertheless, on the positive side, Napster and all future file-sharing sites, plus the legal streaming platforms that are around today, permitted more eyes and ears onto the Red Hot Chili Peppers. Before the internet, artists relied on their internal fan bases to support them through buying their records on CD, vinyl and cassette. But such services back in 1999, whether legal or not, meant anyone who heard 'Scar Tissue' or 'Californication' on the radio and weren't familiar with the Chilis – and who had access to a computer – were more inclined to dig deeper into the band's back catalogue. In 2022, Anthony Kiedis appeared on the *Joe Rogan Experience* podcast, and when discussing those early days of music piracy, the frontman confidently stated how he didn't care if his songs were downloaded illegally – he just wanted people to listen to his band's music. Not all artists share that same sentiment, but it certainly wasn't the worst way to get more people interested in checking out your art.

Californication didn't suffer from piracy because it soared to number three on the *Billboard* 200 on 26 June. Only the Backstreet Boys' *Millennium* and Ricky Martin's self-titled LP prevented the Red Hot Chili Peppers from earning their first number one on the biggest album chart of them all. Incidentally, *Californication* equalled the best placing of *Blood Sugar Sex Magik* from eight years earlier. In the UK, the album reached a highly respectable number five while successfully securing the top spot on the national charts of Australia, Finland, Italy, New Zealand, Norway and Sweden.

Having sold over 16,000,000 copies worldwide, half of which have been from America, *Californication* remains the Red Hot Chili Peppers' most commercially successful record. The continuation in sales during 1999 and 2000 has to be due to the increased publicity of the band and the abundance of press that each member undertook. Every single had a strong promotional campaign, the

Californication Red Hot Chili Peppers

majority of which were accompanied by excellent music videos that received heavy rotation on TV. The intense touring schedule, which included a host of headline festival slots, also played a pivotal role in winning over those who were perhaps less familiar with the band. It also helped that *Californication* was a brilliant album, containing what some reviews stated to be the Chilis' most accomplished music (as of 1999).

Californication did have its criticism, too, though. One sticking point revolved around a lack of the band's signature heavy funk, with only a handful of tracks dialling into the sound that made them famous in the first place. Another negative regarded the overindulgence of mentioning California, even though the state and the areas in it supplied one of the album's overriding themes. The biggest area of cynicism, where many of the complaints came from the band's own fans, surrounded the album's audio inefficiencies. *Californication* has, over the years, been branded the 'worst-ever sounding record' and a 'poster child for the loudness wars'. The term 'loudness wars' comes from what was considered a trend dating as far back as the 1940s. A method by which increasing audio levels of recorded music leads to a reduction in audio fidelity and ultimately decreases a listener's overall enjoyment, the issue became more prominent again in the 1990s with the arrival of the compact disc. At the request of the Red Hot Chili Peppers and Rick Rubin, mastering engineer Vlado Meller used the advances in technology to increase the loudness of *Californication* even further through the use of digital signal processing. Once the maximum amplitude of the CD was reached, loudness was increased through such techniques as dynamic range compression and equalisation, and thus ultimately sacrificed the overall sound quality for loudness. From the very beginning of the album's opening track, the sound compression and distortion is evident for all to hear, with barely any difference coming between the quieter and louder parts. It wasn't long before fans were drawing up online petitions in an attempt to get Warner. Bros Records to remaster the album. But, thanks to that wonderful new thing called file sharing, an unmastered version soon leaked online. The tracks are believed to have been sourced from a CD made up of rough mixes from the Village Recorder sessions and thus contained far less digital distortion. A number of fans speaking online have made clear their preference for these mixes over the originally released tracks.

In 2012, *Californication* was given a vinyl reissue with a fresh master by Chris Bellman and Bernie Grundman. Interestingly, what was considered the best-sounding retail version of the album featured alternative mixes of certain songs. 'Californication' includes traces of organ in the first verse, and there is only one run-through of the first chorus instead of the two included on all other mixes of the title track. 'Easily' features additional vocals during its outro, while one of the verses heard on other iterations of 'Savior' is missing here. It appeared that these versions had been cut from the rough mixes, while the rest of the songs had been taken from the original and official release. But the upgrade in sound quality across the reissue was enough to pacify those who had always loved the album but found it hard to listen to without gaining a headache in the process. In 2024, to celebrate its 25th anniversary, *Californication* was given its first official colour vinyl release, with one red disc and one described as ocean blue. With some considering it the perfect time to give the album a long overdue remaster, it seems Warner Bros. dropped the ball because the vinyl still contains the original mix.

The Legacy Of Californication

There has long been a debate – that will probably continue until the end of time – on which Red Hot Chili Peppers album is the best. Incredibly, it wasn't until 2002 that the quartet secured their first number-one record in either the UK or the US – considered the two most significant charting countries. It was in the UK that *By The Way* began a three-album run of chart-toppers, with *Stadium Arcadium* following in 2006 and then *I'm With You* five years later. More surprisingly, only *Stadium Arcadium,* featuring over 120 minutes of music spread across two CDs (or four vinyl discs, if that is your preference), and 2022's *Unlimited Love* have topped the *Billboard* 200 in America. This has, however, occurred in a day and age where physical sales have dwindled and digital streaming now counts towards chart placings.

But back in 1991, when *Blood Sugar Sex Magik* was released, and in 1999, when *Californication* received its grand unveiling, it was all about those physical sales. This led both albums to become the Chilis' most successful, with *Californication* leading the way at almost 16,000,000 copies sold worldwide. In America, the album sold its first million copies within six weeks of release, and a year later, it was already approaching 4,000,000. On 6 June 2024, *Californication* hit the 8,000,000 mark. All six singles have also been certified, with 'Around The World', 'Parallel Universe' and 'Road Trippin'' going gold for shifting 500,000 units. 'Otherside' went five times platinum, while 'Scar Tissue' and the incomparable title track have gone one better and sold 6,000,000 copies each. Those are some Red Hot statistics, and remember, these are only based on sales within the US.

Blood Sugar Sex Magik has also done some crazy numbers. The album itself has sold close to 12,000,000 worldwide, and in America, it currently stands at seven times platinum. Its last certification came in April 2001, so it's possible that it, too, will hit 8,000,000 before long. The album's biggest single, 'Under The Bridge', is predictably the best-selling of the four that were released, having moved over 6,000,000 copies.

It is these two LPs that both fans and music critics tend to hold in the highest regard. *Blood Sugar Sex Magik* is arguably the Red Hot Chili Peppers' most important record. 'Under The Bridge' was the song to propel the band to worldwide acclaim, while 'Give It Away' and 'Suck My Kiss' revealed an infectious funk-rock formula that finally made audiences sit up and pay attention. Fans often cite the album's tracklisting as being more consistent and flowing in comparison to the latter in this discussion. The 1991 release is also more culturally significant, as it arrived at a time when the alt rock boom was really taking shape and proposed something to run alongside Nirvana, Pearl Jam, Soundgarden and Smashing Pumpkins, who were leading the newly formed grunge movement.

So, if *Blood Sugar Sex Magik* announced their true arrival, *Californication* could be considered the album that saved and resurrected the Red Hot Chili Peppers. Anthony Kiedis did suffer some minor relapses after the album dropped, but his troubles with addiction were largely and thankfully behind him. John Frusciante signified the band's revitalisation, and by moving away from their funk roots and into a more melodic and mature direction, *Californication* presented a band who were bypassing any potential midlife crisis and choosing a sharper focus that would enable them to become one of the biggest bands on the planet. In the 2000s, it certainly seemed like the quartet had never been so damn popular.

In an interview with *Guitarworld* in July 1999, Chad Smith spoke of how the success of *Californication* was largely down to the band's ability to quickly return to their old ways of writing songs:

> There is no one way that the songs start. We just get over to Flea's, sit down and start playing. Just jam. Lots of songs came out of that, and that's something, I think, that was lacking when we were working with Dave (Navarro). He's more of a reactive guitar player – he puts parts to stuff that already exists.
>
> With us, it's just chemistry between the four of us, and there's never any one way that it happens. Like, Flea might have been sitting at home, and he'll come up with a bass part. So he'll say, 'What do you guys think of this?' And we'll fall in and start playing. Or John, the same thing.
>
> There are no preconceived plans, no 'We're gonna write a funky song today'. Or a slow song. Or a fast song. It's just however we're feeling that day, that's what comes up. It's the most natural way to do it, and a big part of why the album sounds the way it does is because it's not forced.

John Frusciante echoed Smith's sentiments in the same interview:

> In this band, we have this thing where each one of us has our reasons for playing music, and they somehow all fit together. I mean, the reason I started playing music was because of punk rock

and new wave. And the reason that Flea started playing music was because of Louie Armstrong and jazz people. But because of what he's grown into and what I've grown into, we're playing music for very similar reasons. When we each hold our instrument, we're trying to do a very similar thing but in a different way. So when we're all getting along, we're capable of making really good music.

At the 2000 Grammy Awards, the Red Hot Chili Peppers earned three nominations for their latest work. *Californication* was put forward for Best Rock Album and 'Scar Tissue' received two nods in the Best Rock Performance and Best Rock Song categories. The hit single successfully scooped the latter award, and thus, the Chilis' second prestigious Grammy. A year later, the title track was the one nominated for Best Rock Performance and Best Rock Song, and although it won neither award, the fact it had been selected in the first place confirmed that, after 18 months of being out there in the ether, *Californication* and its excellent set of songs was still receiving a lot of mainstream attention. Elsewhere, *Californication* won Best Album at the MTV Europe Awards and the Chilis won Favourite Alternative Artist and Best International Group at the American Music Awards and the Brit Awards, respectively.

In 2003, *Rolling Stone* curated a list of their 500 Greatest Albums of All Time, and Californication was included at number 399. In a revised 2024 edition, it had climbed to 286. *Q* magazine produced its own 250 Best Albums countdown in 2011, in which *Blood Sugar Sex Magik* landed at 126 and *Californication* came in at 42. Both albums have also been featured in Robert Dimery's weighty anthology book *1001 Albums You Must Hear Before You Die*, but most illustriously of all, they are part of the Rock & Roll Hall of Fame's Definitive 200. Alongside music royalty such as The Beatles, Prince, Bruce Springsteen, Elton John and Queen, the 2007 announcement of the Top 200 Albums of All Time saw *Blood Sugar Sex Magik* ranked at 88 and *Californication* just behind it at 92. The criteria to make the list were based on sales performance and potential lasting popularity.

Five years later, the Red Hot Chili Peppers were inducted into the Rock & Roll Hall of Fame and thus cemented their legacy as one of the best and most popular rock bands in history. Their legend increased even more when the quartet were awarded a star on the Hollywood Walk of Fame in 2022. The Chilis had finally been acknowledged by their adopted hometown for their achievements, contributions and musical longevity. Ahead of them revealing their star, each member of the band spoke briefly in front of proud fans and musical alumni. Anthony Kiedis spoke last and most passionately as he perfectly summed up the bond the four had forged over the years and how, even through their darkest periods, that bond has more than stood the test of time:

> To me, this is not a story of individuals. I love Chad, I love Flea and I love John greatly. They're amazingly talented. Flea's at one with the bass, John is my favourite guitar player of all time and Chad Smith is the finest drummer in the land. But really, something happens when we come together, which is much greater than the individual parts. The sum total of our parts is that we were able to find something that we love doing and communicate with the entire world.

Bibliography

Audio
Bill Hicks – 'Arizona Bay' (Rykodisc, 1997)
The Joe Rogan Experience Podcast
Rick Rubin's Broken Record Podcast

Books
Kiedis, A., *Scar Tissue* (Hyperion, 2004)
Dimery, R., *1001 Albums You Must Hear Before You Die* (Universe Publishing, 2005)

Video
Woodstock '99: Peace, Love & Rage (HBO, 2021)
YouTube.com

Websites
Albumism.com
Billboard.com
Diffuser.fm
Everythingisnoise.net
Genius.com
Guitar.com
Guitarworld.com
Kerrang.com
Loudersound.com
Mixdownmag.com.au
Nme.com
Pitchfork.com
Radiox.co.uk
Redhotchilipeppers.com
Rhcplivearchive.com
Rhcpsessions.com
Riaa.com
Rockaxis.com
Rockhall.com
Rollingstone.com
Setlist.fm
Songfacts.com
Soundonsound.com
Stereogum.com
Thisisdig.com
Walkoffame.com

Also available from Sonicbond

On Track Series

Allman Brothers Band – Andrew Wild 978-1-78952-252-5
Tori Amos – Lisa Torem 978-1-78952-142-9
Aphex Twin – Beau Waddell 978-1-78952-267-9
Asia – Peter Braidis 978-1-78952-099-6
Badfinger – Robert Day-Webb 978-1-878952-176-4
Barclay James Harvest – Keith And Monica Domone 978-1-78952-067-5
Beck – Arthur Lizie 978-1-78952-258-7
The Beatles – Andrew Wild 978-1-78952-009-5
The Beatles Solo 1969-1980 – Andrew Wild 978-1-78952-030-9
Blue Oyster Cult – Jacob Holm-Lupo 978-1-78952-007-1
Blur – Matt Bishop 978-178952-164-1
Marc Bolan And T.rex – Peter Gallagher 978-1-78952-124-5
Kate Bush – Bill Thomas 978-1-78952-097-2
Camel – Hamish Kuzminski 978-1-78952-040-8
Captain Beefheart – Opher Goodwin 978-1-78952-235-8
Caravan – Andy Boot 978-1-78952-127-6
Cardiacs – Eric Benac 978-1-78952-131-3
Nick Cave And The Bad Seeds – Dominic Sanderson 978-1-78952-240-2
Eric Clapton Solo – Andrew Wild 978-1-78952-141-2
The Clash – Nick Assirati 978-1-78952-077-4
Elvis Costello And The Attractions – Georg Purvis 978-1-78952-129-0
Crosby, Stills And Nash – Andrew Wild 978-1-78952-039-2
Creedence Clearwater Revival – Tony Thompson 978-178952-237-2
The Damned – Morgan Brown 978-1-78952-136-8
Deep Purple And Rainbow 1968-79 – Steve Pilkington 978-1-78952-002-6
Dire Straits – Andrew Wild 978-1-78952-044-6
The Doors – Tony Thompson 978-1-78952-137-5
Dream Theater – Jordan Blum 978-1-78952-050-7
Eagles – John Van Der Kiste 978-1-78952-260-0
Earth, Wind And Fire – Bud Wilkins 978-1-78952-272-3
Electric Light Orchestra – Barry Delve 978-1-78952-152-8
Emerson Lake And Palmer – Mike Goode 978-1-78952-000-2
Fairport Convention – Kevan Furbank 978-1-78952-051-4
Peter Gabriel – Graeme Scarfe 978-1-78952-138-2
Genesis – Stuart Macfarlane 978-1-78952-005-7
Gentle Giant – Gary Steel 978-1-78952-058-3

Also available from Sonicbond

Gong – Kevan Furbank 978-1-78952-082-8
Green Day – William E. Spevack 978-1-78952-261-7
Hall And Oates – Ian Abrahams 978-1-78952-167-2
Hawkwind – Duncan Harris 978-1-78952-052-1
Peter Hammill – Richard Rees Jones 978-1-78952-163-4
Roy Harper – Opher Goodwin 978-1-78952-130-6
Jimi Hendrix – Emma Stott 978-1-78952-175-7
The Hollies – Andrew Darlington 978-1-78952-159-7
Horslips – Richard James 978-1-78952-263-1
The Human League And The Sheffield Scene – Andrew Darlington 978-1-78952-186-3
The Incredible String Band – Tim Moon 978-1-78952-107-8
Iron Maiden – Steve Pilkington 978-1-78952-061-3
Joe Jackson – Richard James 978-1-78952-189-4
Jefferson Airplane – Richard Butterworth 978-1-78952-143-6
Jethro Tull – Jordan Blum 978-1-78952-016-3
Elton John In The 1970s – Peter Kearns 978-1-78952-034-7
Billy Joel – Lisa Torem 978-1-78952-183-2
Judas Priest – John Tucker 978-1-78952-018-7
Kansas – Kevin Cummings 978-1-78952-057-6
The Kinks – Martin Hutchinson 978-1-78952-172-6
Korn – Matt Karpe 978-1-78952-153-5
Led Zeppelin – Steve Pilkington 978-1-78952-151-1
Level 42 – Matt Philips 978-1-78952-102-3
Little Feat – Georg Purvis - 978-1-78952-168-9
Aimee Mann – Jez Rowden 978-1-78952-036-1
Joni Mitchell – Peter Kearns 978-1-78952-081-1
The Moody Blues – Geoffrey Feakes 978-1-78952-042-2
Motorhead – Duncan Harris 978-1-78952-173-3
Nektar – Scott Meze – 978-1-78952-257-0
New Order – Dennis Remmer – 978-1-78952-249-5
Nightwish – Simon Mcmurdo – 978-1-78952-270-9
Laura Nyro – Philip Ward 978-1-78952-182-5
Mike Oldfield – Ryan Yard 978-1-78952-060-6
Opeth – Jordan Blum 978-1-78-952-166-5
Pearl Jam – Ben L. Connor 978-1-78952-188-7
Tom Petty – Richard James 978-1-78952-128-3
Pink Floyd – Richard Butterworth 978-1-78952-242-6
The Police – Pete Braidis 978-1-78952-158-0
Porcupine Tree – Nick Holmes 978-1-78952-144-3

Also available from Sonicbond

Queen – Andrew Wild 978-1-78952-003-3
Radiohead – William Allen 978-1-78952-149-8
Rancid – Paul Matts 989-1-78952-187-0
Renaissance – David Detmer 978-1-78952-062-0
Reo Speedwagon – Jim Romag 978-1-78952-262-4
The Rolling Stones 1963-80 – Steve Pilkington 978-1-78952-017-0
The Smiths And Morrissey – Tommy Gunnarsson 978-1-78952-140-5
Spirit – Rev. Keith A. Gordon – 978-1-78952- 248-8
Stackridge – Alan Draper 978-1-78952-232-7
Status Quo The Frantic Four Years – Richard James 978-1-78952-160-3
Steely Dan – Jez Rowden 978-1-78952-043-9
Steve Hackett – Geoffrey Feakes 978-1-78952-098-9
Tears For Fears – Paul Clark - 978-178952-238-9
Thin Lizzy – Graeme Stroud 978-1-78952-064-4
Tool – Matt Karpe 978-1-78952-234-1
Toto – Jacob Holm-Lupo 978-1-78952-019-4
U2 – Eoghan Lyng 978-1-78952-078-1
Ufo – Richard James 978-1-78952-073-6
Van Der Graaf Generator – Dan Coffey 978-1-78952-031-6
Van Halen – Morgan Brown – 9781-78952-256-3
The Who – Geoffrey Feakes 978-1-78952-076-7
Roy Wood And The Move – James R Turner 978-1-78952-008-8
Yes – Stephen Lambe 978-1-78952-001-9
Frank Zappa 1966 To 1979 – Eric Benac 978-1-78952-033-0
Warren Zevon – Peter Gallagher 978-1-78952-170-2
10cc – Peter Kearns 978-1-78952-054-5

Decades Series
The Bee Gees In The 1960s – Andrew Mon Hughes Et Al 978-1-78952-148-1
The Bee Gees In The 1970s – Andrew Mon Hughes Et Al 978-1-78952-179-5
Black Sabbath In The 1970s – Chris Sutton 978-1-78952-171-9
Britpop – Peter Richard Adams And Matt Pooler 978-1-78952-169-6
Phil Collins In The 1980s – Andrew Wild 978-1-78952-185-6
Alice Cooper In The 1970s – Chris Sutton 978-1-78952-104-7
Alice Cooper In The 1980s – Chris Sutton 978-1-78952-259-4
Curved Air In The 1970s – Laura Shenton 978-1-78952-069-9

Also available from Sonicbond

Donovan In The 1960s – Jeff Fitzgerald 978-1-78952-233-4
Bob Dylan In The 1980s – Don Klees 978-1-78952-157-3
Brian Eno In The 1970s – Gary Parsons 978-1-78952-239-6
Faith No More In The 1990s – Matt Karpe 978-1-78952-250-1
Fleetwood Mac In The 1970s – Andrew Wild 978-1-78952-105-4
Fleetwood Mac In The 1980s – Don Klees 978-178952-254-9
Focus In The 1970s – Stephen Lambe 978-1-78952-079-8
Free And Bad Company In The 1970s – John Van Der Kiste 978-1-78952-178-8
Genesis In The 1970s – Bill Thomas 978178952-146-7
George Harrison In The 1970s – Eoghan Lyng 978-1-78952-174-0
Kiss In The 1970s – Peter Gallagher 978-1-78952-246-4
Manfred Mann's Earth Band In The 1970s – John Van Der Kiste 978178952-243-3
Marillion In The 1980s – Nathaniel Webb 978-1-78952-065-1
Van Morrison In The 1970s – Peter Childs - 978-1-78952-241-9
Mott The Hoople And Ian Hunter In The 1970s –
John Van Der Kiste 978-1-78-952-162-7
Pink Floyd In The 1970s – Georg Purvis 978-1-78952-072-9
Suzi Quatro In The 1970s – Darren Johnson 978-1-78952-236-5
Queen In The 1970s – James Griffiths 978-1-78952-265-5
Roxy Music In The 1970s – Dave Thompson 978-1-78952-180-1
Slade In The 1970s – Darren Johnson 978-1-78952-268-6
Status Quo In The 1980s – Greg Harper 978-1-78952-244-0
Tangerine Dream In The 1970s – Stephen Palmer 978-1-78952-161-0
The Sweet In The 1970s – Darren Johnson 978-1-78952-139-9
Uriah Heep In The 1970s – Steve Pilkington 978-1-78952-103-0
Van Der Graaf Generator In The 1970s – Steve Pilkington 978-1-78952-245-7
Rick Wakeman In The 1970s – Geoffrey Feakes 978-1-78952-264-8
Yes In The 1980s – Stephen Lambe With David Watkinson 978-1-78952-125-2

On Screen Series
Carry On... – Stephen Lambe 978-1-78952-004-0
David Cronenberg – Patrick Chapman 978-1-78952-071-2
Doctor Who: The David Tennant Years – Jamie Hailstone 978-1-78952-066-8
James Bond – Andrew Wild 978-1-78952-010-1

Also available from Sonicbond

Monty Python – Steve Pilkington 978-1-78952-047-7
Seinfeld Seasons 1 To 5 – Stephen Lambe 978-1-78952-012-5

Other Books

1967: A Year In Psychedelic Rock – Kevan Furbank
978-1-78952-155-9
1970: A Year In Rock – John Van Der Kiste 978-1-78952-147-4
1973: The Golden Year Of Progressive Rock – Geoffrey Feakes
978-1-78952-165-8
Babysitting A Band On The Rocks – G.D. Praetorius
978-1-78952-106-1
Eric Clapton Sessions – Andrew Wild 978-1-78952-177-1
Derek Taylor: For Your Radioactive Children –
Andrew Darlington 978-1-78952-038-5
The Golden Road: The Recording History Of The Grateful Dead –
John Kilbride 978-1-78952-156-6
Iggy And The Stooges On Stage 1967-1974 – Per Nilsen
978-1-78952-101-6
Jon Anderson And The Warriors – The Road To Yes –
David Watkinson 978-1-78952-059-0
Magic: The David Paton Story – David Paton 978-1-78952-266-2
Misty: The Music Of Johnny Mathis – Jakob Baekgaard
978-1-78952-247-1
Nu Metal: A Definitive Guide – Matt Karpe 978-1-78952-063-7
Tommy Bolin: In And Out Of Deep Purple – Laura Shenton
978-1-78952-070-5
Maximum Darkness – Deke Leonard 978-1-78952-048-4
The Twang Dynasty – Deke Leonard 978-1-78952-049-1

and many more to come!

Would you like to write for Sonicbond Publishing?

We are mainly a music publisher, but we also occasionally publish in other genres including film and television. At Sonicbond Publishing we are always on the look-out for authors, particularly for our two main series, On Track and Decades.

Mixing fact with in depth analysis, the On Track series examines the entire recorded work of a particular musical artist or group. All genres are considered from easy listening and jazz to 60s soul to 90s pop, via rock and metal.

The Decades series singles out a particular decade in an artist or group's history and focuses on that decade in more detail than may be allowed in the On Track series.

While professional writing experience would, of course, be an advantage, the most important qualification is to have real enthusiasm and knowledge of your subject. First-time authors are welcomed, but the ability to write well in English is essential.

Sonicbond Publishing has distribution throughout Europe and North America, and all our books are also published in E-book form. Authors will be paid a royalty based on sales of their book.

Further details about our books are available from www.sonicbondpublishing.com. To contact us, complete the contact form there or email info@sonicbondpublishing.co.uk